LONELY PLANET

BIGGER
BOOK

of

EVERYTHING

A Visual Guide to Travel & the World

NIGEL HOLMES

**To Erin, with love to the
best travel partner anyone could
possibly wish for.**

THE

LONELY PLANET

BIGGER
BOOK

of

EVERYTHING

A Visual Guide to Travel & the World

NIGEL HOLMES

CONTENTS

CONTENTS

Foreword

Dear Reader, please be aware that even though this is its second edition, *The Book of Everything* still doesn't have **everything** in it. (For that, you'll have to wait until, um, perhaps the 20th edition?)

So there's nothing about a whole lot of stuff that you might like to know before or during your travel exploits. No mention of how to build an igloo in Alaska; nothing about how to pack for a trip to Anjalankoski*; not a word on Montezuma's Revenge in Mexico. Oh well, we worked hard to make what *is* here as relevant and interesting as we could.

This appears on every page. If you are reading with a dirty left thumb, make sure your thumb goes right here. That way, you won't mess up the pages.

Although the book was written and drawn with a light-hearted touch, several pages, especially some in the health and safety section, deal with serious subjects for travellers. I'm a lifelong designer of infographics—explaining things—but am by no means an expert in medical or security matters, so the health and safety pages were some of the most demanding for me to produce. They required a level of research and attention to detail that was different to, for instance, gathering facts about the world's longest rivers and highest mountains, or describing how snow forms, or showing the proper way to wear the kilt. So while I'm not sure that I would volunteer to deliver a baby in an emergency, nor dare to perform a tracheotomy, it's all in here.

It seemed fitting for a book that's a collection of infographics to do a graphic about how a typical two-page spread was made. Here it is... ⟶

* It's in Finland. Look it up.

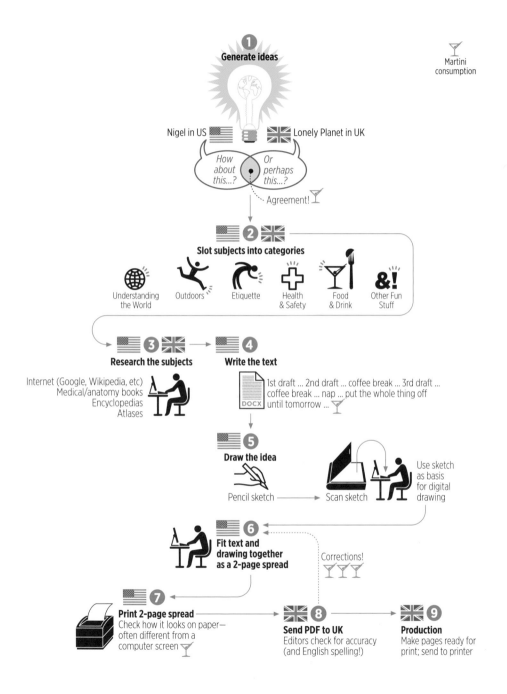

1 Generate ideas

Martini consumption

Nigel in US — Lonely Planet in UK

How about this...? Or perhaps this...?

Agreement!

2 Slot subjects into categories

Understanding the World — Outdoors — Etiquette — Health & Safety — Food & Drink — Other Fun Stuff

3 Research the subjects

Internet (Google, Wikipedia, etc)
Medical/anatomy books
Encyclopedias
Atlases

4 Write the text

1st draft ... 2nd draft ... coffee break ... 3rd draft ... coffee break ... nap ... put the whole thing off until tomorrow ...

5 Draw the idea

Pencil sketch ⟶ Scan sketch — Use sketch as basis for digital drawing

6 Fit text and drawing together as a 2-page spread

Corrections!

7 Print 2-page spread
Check how it looks on paper—often different from a computer screen

8 Send PDF to UK
Editors check for accuracy (and English spelling!)

9 Production
Make pages ready for print; send to printer

UNDERSTANDING THE WORLD

A different world

What's a travel book without a map of the world? And why
do we always look at it the same way? This view might help you
to see countries in a new light. (Then again it might just be totally annoying.)

New
Zealand

*It's great
to be at the top
for a change!*

Australia

Pacific
Islands

Singapore

Papua
New
Guinea

I n d o n e s i a

Malaysia

Brunei

Philippines

Vietnam

Hong Kong

Taiwan

Laos

Myanmar

Japan

S. Korea

N. Korea

China

Mongolia

Russia

Cambodia
Thailand

Bangladesh

Sri Lanka

India

Nepal

Bhutan

Pakistan

Tajikistan

Afghanistan

Turkmenistan

Uzbekistan

Kazakhstan

Azerbaijan

Armenia

*Some
smaller countries
haven't been named.*

Mauritius

Tanzania

Djibouti
Eritrea

Palestine
Jordan
Bahrain
Oman
Lebanon

Madagascar

Burundi
Rwanda
Uganda

Kenya

Somalia

Ethiopia

UAE Saudi
Arabia
Kuwait
Iraq
Iran
Syria

Turkey

Lesotho

eSwatini

Mozambique

Malawi

South Africa

Namibia

Zimbabwe

Botswana

Zambia

Angola

Congo
Gabon
Equatorial Guinea

Dem. Rep.
of Congo

Benin
Cameroon Togo

Central
African
Republic

South
Sudan

Nigeria

Ivory Coast

Liberia

Ghana

Burkina Guinea
Faso

Sierra Leone
Guinea-
Bissau
Gamb...

Sudan

Chad

Niger

Mali Mauritania

Senega...

Egypt

Libya

Algeria

Western
Sahara

Morocco

Israel
Cyprus

North
Macedonia Tunisia
Albania

Greece Italy

Bulgaria Serbia
Romania
Moldova

Croatia

Austria

Ukraine

Belarus

Germany

Poland

Lithuania Denmark
Latvia
Estonia

Finland

Sweden

Czech Republic
Slovakia
Hungary

Spain

Portugal

France

Switzerland

Ireland

United Kingdom

Belgium
Netherlands

Norway

Iceland

Uruguay
Chile
Argentina
Paraguay
Bolivia
Peru
Brazil
Guyana
Ecuador
French Guiana
Suriname
Colombia
Costa Rica
Panama
Venezuela
Nicaragua
El Salvador
Jamaica
Guatemala
Caribbean Islands
Puerto Rico
Haiti
Honduras
Dominican Rep.
Cuba
Belize
Mexico
Bahamas
Bermuda
Hawaii →
United States
Canada
Greenland

Is it really upside down?

Our custom of orienting maps with north at the top is arbitrary. The Greek cartographer and astronomer Ptolemy drew his maps that way around the year AD 150, and most mapmakers have followed his example.

Some people think that north-oriented maps have an implicit bias toward the northern hemisphere, and many classic (and still used) world projections do favour the northern hemisphere. This is because at the time these maps were made, most of the developed world was in the north and more room was needed to show the detail in this area.

When the famous photo of Earth taken from space (aboard Apollo 17) was first published, in 1972, it showed the South Pole like this:

That's Africa, or rather, Africa.

NASA

Publications quickly turned the image round to fit the established convention.

Around the world: the equator

The first person to sail around the globe was Juan Sebastián del Cano, who took credit after his captain, Ferdinand Magellan, was killed en route. The voyage lasted almost 3 years, from 1519 to 1522.

In 1961, Russian cosmonaut Yuri Gagarin was the first to make the trip into space. It took 1 hour and 48 minutes.

EQUATOR

PACIFIC OCEAN

You can set foot on only about 8000km (5000 miles; 20%) of the Equator's length, **in the places shown in red.**

The Pacific Ocean alone accounts for 18,000km (about 11,000 miles) of water around the middle of the Earth.

Galápagos Islands

Ecuador

Colombia

Brazil

Malaku (Moluccas)
Sulawesi (Celebes)
Borneo

Sumatra

Maldives

ATLANTIC OCEAN

INDIAN OCEAN

Dem. Republic of Congo

Gabon
Congo
Uganda
Kenya
Somalia

Equator days are the same year round: 12 hours of daylight, 12 of darkness. The sun rises around 6am and sets around 6pm.

Global climate change has special urgency in the **Maldives.** If the sea level continues rising at current rates, most of the 1200 islands and atolls will be under water by 2100, according to the UN.

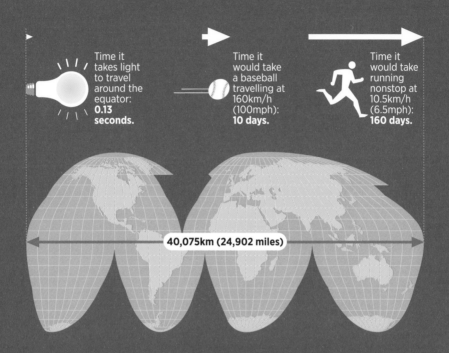

Time it takes light to travel around the equator: **0.13 seconds.**

Time it would take a baseball travelling at 160km/h (100mph): **10 days.**

Time it would take running nonstop at 10.5km/h (6.5mph): **160 days.**

40,075km (24,902 miles)

Why it's so darn hot

It's hot almost everywhere on the equator because the sun's rays hit the earth there straight on, heating the ground and the air above it. Elsewhere, the rays hit the atmosphere at an angle because the earth is curved. This dissipates some of the sun's energy.

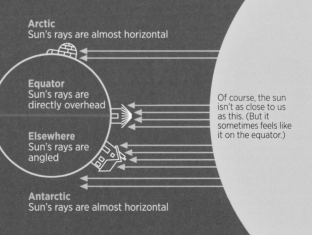

Arctic
Sun's rays are almost horizontal

Equator
Sun's rays are directly overhead

Elsewhere
Sun's rays are angled

Antarctic
Sun's rays are almost horizontal

Of course, the sun isn't as close to us as this. (But it sometimes feels like it on the equator.)

The world's highest mountains

The really high ones are all in Asia. Shown here are Asia's top five.

(There are 60 other peaks in Asia that are higher than the tallest in South America, below.)

The top of **Asia**

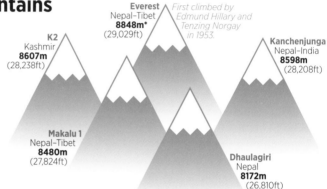

Everest
Nepal–Tibet
8848m*
(29,029ft)

First climbed by Edmund Hillary and Tenzing Norgay in 1953.

K2
Kashmir
8607m
(28,238ft)

Kanchenjunga
Nepal–India
8598m
(28,208ft)

Makalu 1
Nepal–Tibet
8480m
(27,824ft)

Dhaulagiri
Nepal
8172m
(26,810ft)

The top of **South America**

Aconcagua
Argentina
6959m
(22,834ft)

Ojos del Salado
Argentina–Chile
6880m
(22,572ft)

Bonete
Argentina
6872m
(22,546ft)

Pissis
Argentina
6793m
(22,287ft)

The top of **North America**

Denali (McKinley)
USA
6194m
(20,320ft)

Logan
Canada
6050m
(19,850ft)

Citlaltépetl
Mexico
5700m
(18,700ft)

The top of **Africa**

Kilimanjaro
Tanzania
5895m
(19,340ft)

Kenya
Kenya
5199m
(17,058ft)

Margherita Peak
Uganda
5109m
(16,763ft)

The top of **Europe**

Mont Blanc
France–Italy
4807m
(15,771ft)

Monte Rosa
Switzerland
4634m
(15,203ft)

Dom
Switzerland
4545m
(14,911ft)

*The height of a mountain (including Everest) is hard to pin down. Some sources cite the height of the rock as the top, others include the ice and snow above the rock, which changes with the seasons. Nepal is planning a new survey of Everest.

And the longest rivers

Nile Africa **6670km** (4145 miles)

Amazon South America **6437km** (4000 miles)

Yangtze Asia **6300km** (3914 miles)

Mississippi–Missouri North America **5971km** (3710 miles)

Yenisey–Angara Asia **5539km** (3441 miles)

Yellow Asia **5464km** (3395 miles)

Ob–Irtysh Asia **5411km** (3362 miles)

Paraná South America **4880km** (3362 miles)

Congo Africa **4667km** (2900 miles)

Amur–Heilong Asia **4467km** (2774 miles)

Lena Asia **4400km** (2734 miles)

Mekong Asia **4350km** (2702 miles)

Mackenzie–Peace North America **4241km** (2635 miles)

What are the "Northern Lights"?

Properly known as the **Aurora Borealis,** they are a wonderful sight that lights up the northern night sky. (Aurora was the Roman goddess of dawn; Boreas is the Greek name for the north wind.) Here's the science behind what you see.

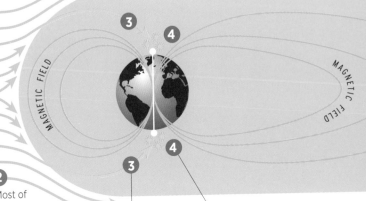

1 Streams of charged particles (electrons and protons) flow from the sun to Earth at a velocity of over 1.4 million km/h (900,000 mph).

2 Most of the particles are deflected by Earth's magnetosphere, (shown here in light blue ...)

3 but some are sucked into the vortex of Earth's magnetic fields (pink lines) at the North and South Poles. (In the south, the effect is called **Aurora Australis,** or the Southern Lights.)

4 What we see as an aurora is the interaction of those charged particles with atoms from Earth's atmosphere. They form an oval ring around each pole.

Shown here is one type of aurora, which appears like billowing curtains hanging in the air. (The other common effect is a diffuse glow swirling across the sky.) Auroras vary in colour from fluorescent greens to soft reds and yellows.

Where (and when) are the best places to view the "lights"?
Wherever you are, you need a clear, dark sky.
The best time is around midnight in winter.

To see the Aurora Borealis in the **north,** go to Alaska, Canada, Greenland, Iceland, Scandinavia and the northern coast of Siberia.

To see the Aurora Australis in the **south,** your best bets are Antarctica, South America, Tasmania and the southern tip of New Zealand.

What do those signs mean?

How to read the signals that the guy on the runway is giving to your pilot.
(They're called marshalling signals.)

start engines

move ahead

turn to your left

turn to your right

all clear

this way

slow down

stop

The world's most commonly spoken languages

Each 🗨 = 10,000 speakers

Mandarin (spoken in 5 countries)
🗨🗨

English (115 countries)   **480 million** speakers
🗨🗨

Spanish (20 countries)   **320 million**
🗨🗨🗨🗨🗨🗨🗨🗨🗨🗨🗨🗨🗨🗨🗨🗨🗨🗨🗨🗨🗨🗨🗨🗨🗨🗨🗨🗨🗨🗨🗨🗨

Russian (16 countries)   **285 million**
🗨🗨🗨🗨🗨🗨🗨🗨🗨🗨🗨🗨🗨🗨🗨🗨🗨🗨🗨🗨🗨🗨🗨🗨🗨🗨🗨🗨

French (35 countries)   **265 million**
🗨🗨🗨🗨🗨🗨🗨🗨🗨🗨🗨🗨🗨🗨🗨🗨🗨🗨🗨🗨🗨🗨🗨🗨🗨🗨

Hindi/Urdu (2 countries)   **250 million**
🗨🗨🗨🗨🗨🗨🗨🗨🗨🗨🗨🗨🗨🗨🗨🗨🗨🗨🗨🗨🗨🗨🗨🗨🗨

Arabic (24 countries)   **221 million**
🗨🗨🗨🗨🗨🗨🗨🗨🗨🗨🗨🗨🗨🗨🗨🗨🗨🗨🗨🗨🗨🗨

Portuguese (5 countries)   **188 million**
🗨🗨🗨🗨🗨🗨🗨🗨🗨🗨🗨🗨🗨🗨🗨🗨🗨🗨🗨

Bengali (1 country)   **185 million**
🗨🗨🗨🗨🗨🗨🗨🗨🗨🗨🗨🗨🗨🗨🗨🗨🗨🗨🗨

Japanese (1 country)   **133 million**
🗨🗨🗨🗨🗨🗨🗨🗨🗨🗨🗨🗨🗨🗨

German (9 countries) **109 million**
🗨🗨🗨🗨🗨🗨🗨🗨🗨🗨🗨

If you go to a country where you don't know
a word of the language, *Google Translate*
can help. It's free, has 100 languages, and
is available on iOS and Android smartphones.

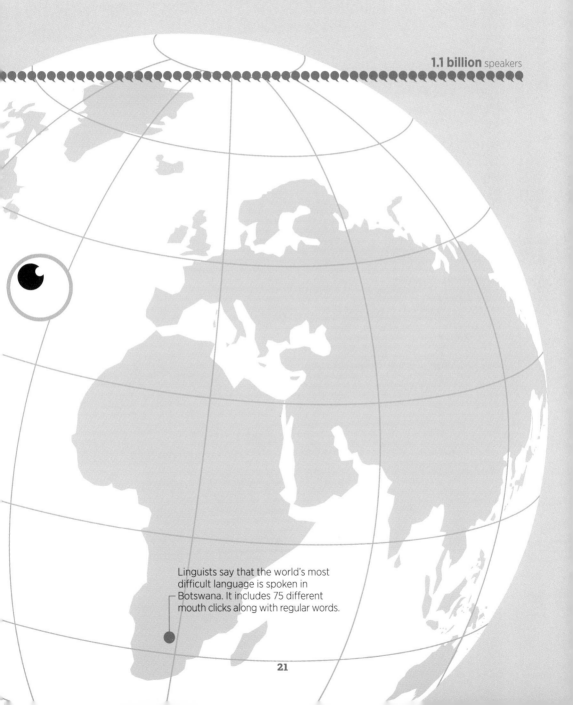

1.1 billion speakers

Linguists say that the world's most difficult language is spoken in Botswana. It includes 75 different mouth clicks along with regular words.

How to count to 10 in 25 languages

	0	1	2	3	4
Arabic	sifr	wahid	'itnan	talata	'arba'a
Basque	zero	bat	bi	hiru	lau
Cheyenne		na'estse	nese	na'he	neve
Danish	nul	en	to	tre	fire
Dutch	nul	een	twee	drie	vier
Esperanto	nul	unu	du	tri	kvar
French	zéro	un	deux	trois	quatre
Fijian	saiva	dua	rua	tolu	vaa
German	null	eins	zwei	drei	vier
Hindi		ek	do	teen	char
Hungarian	nulla	egy	ketto	harom	negy
Italian	zero	uno	due	tre	quattro
Japanese		ichi	ni	san	shi/yon
Korean		il	i	sam	sa
Mandarin	ling	yi	er/liang	san	si
Norwegian	null	en	to	tre	fire
Persian	sefr	yek	do	se	charhar
Polish	zero	jeden	dwa	trzy	cztery
Portuguese	zero	um	dois	tres	quatro
Russian	nol	odin	dva	tri	cetyre
Spanish	cero	uno	dos	tres	cuatro
Swahili	sifuri	moja	mbili	tatu	nne
Swedish	noll	en	tva	tre	fyra
Turkish	sifir	bir	iki	üç	dört
Zulu	iqanda	kunye	kubili	kuthathu	kune

5	6	7	8	9	10
hamsa	sitta	sab'a	tamaniya	tis'a	'asara
bost	sei	zazpi	zortzi	bederatzi	hamar
noho	naesohto	nesohto	na'nohto	soohto	mahtohto
fem	seks	syv	otte	ni	ti
vijf	zes	zeven	acht	negen	tien
kvir	ses	sep	ok	nau	dek
cinq	six	sept	huit	neuf	dix
lima	ono	vitu	walu	ciwa	tini
funf	sechs	sieben	acht	neun	zehn
panch	che	saath	aath	noh	dus
ot	hat	het	nyolc	kilenc	tiz
cinque	sei	sette	otto	nove	dieci
go	roku	nana/shichi	hachi	ku/kyuu	jyuu
o	yuk	chil	pal	ku	sip
wu	liu	qi	ba	jiu	shi
fem	seks	sju	atte	ni	ti
panj	shesh	haft	hasht	noh	dah
piec	szesc	siedem	osiem	dziewiec	dziesiec
cinco	seis	sete	oito	nove	dez
pjat	sest	sem	vosem	devjat	desjat
cinco	seis	siete	ocho	nueve	diez
tano	sita	saba	nane	tisa	kumi
fem	sex	sju	atta	nio	tio
bes	alti	yedi	sekiz	dokuz	on
ishianu	isithuptha	isikhombisa	isishiya-galombili	isishiya galolunye	ishumi

Can't find the word?
Point! 👉

Mother!

A look at one branch of the **world's language tree,** and how to say "hello" to a particularly important person.

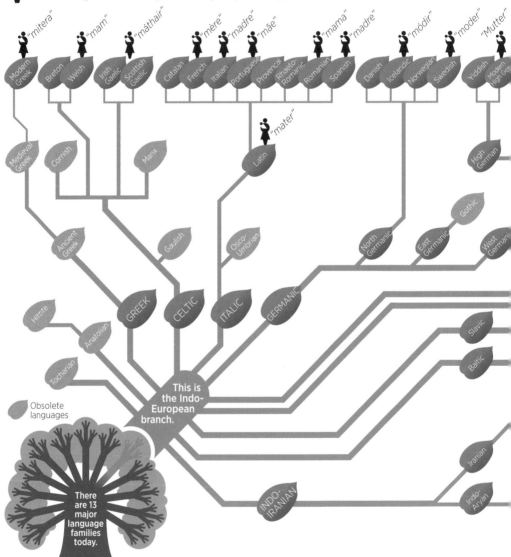

"mitera" — Modern Greek
"mam" — Breton, Welsh
"máthair" — Irish Gaelic, Scottish Gaelic
"mère" — Catalan, French
"madre" — Italian
"mãe" — Portuguese, Provençal, Rhaeto-Romanic
"mama" — Romanian
"madre" — Spanish
"módir" — Danish, Icelandic, Norwegian
"moder" — Swedish
"Mutter" — Yiddish, Modern High German

"mater" — Latin

Medieval Greek, Cornish, Manx, Gaulish, Osco-Umbrian, Latin, High German, North Germanic, East Germanic, Gothic, West Germanic

Ancient Greek, Hittite, Anatolian, Tocharian

GREEK, CELTIC, ITALIC, GERMANIC, Slavic, Baltic

This is the Indo-European branch.

Obsolete languages

There are 13 major language families today.

INDO-IRANIAN, Iranian, Indo-Aryan

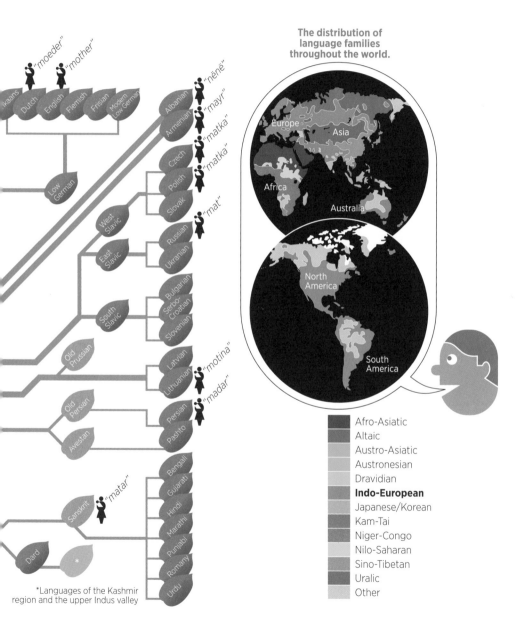

The distribution of language families throughout the world.

"moeder"   "mother"

Afrikaans · Dutch · English · Flemish · Frisian · Modern Low German

Low German

Albanian "nënë"

Armenian "mayr"

Czech "matka"

Polish "matka"

Slovak

West Slavic

Russian "mat"

East Slavic

Ukrainian

Bulgarian

Serbo-Croatian

South Slavic

Slovenian

Old Prussian

Latvian "motina"

Lithuanian

Old Persian

Persian "madar"

Avestan

Pashto

Bengali

Gujarati

Sanskrit "matar"

Hindi

Marathi

Dard

Punjabi

*

Romany

Urdu

*Languages of the Kashmir region and the upper Indus valley

Europe
Asia
Africa
Australia
North America
South America

- Afro-Asiatic
- Altaic
- Austro-Asiatic
- Austronesian
- Dravidian
- **Indo-European**
- Japanese/Korean
- Kam-Tai
- Niger-Congo
- Nilo-Saharan
- Sino-Tibetan
- Uralic
- Other

How to read Egyptian hieroglyphs

(Greek for 'sacred carvings')

It's more complicated than you think. This ancient writing system contains more than **2000 symbols,** some more representational than others. Originating somewhere between 3100 BCE and CE 40, the hieroglyphs were not understood until the 1799 discovery of the **Rosetta Stone** by soldiers in Napoleon's army in the town of Rosetta, Egypt.

The tabletop-sized slab of black rock was covered with texts in three languages: **Egyptian hieroglyphs, Greek and a second Egyptian script.** In 1822, a French language scholar, Jean-François Champollion, finally solved the riddle of the Stone, largely by matching up the pictorial Egyptian hieroglyphs with the readable Greek text.

You can see the Rosetta Stone in the British Museum, in London.

The structure of the language is complex—the signs are divided into three categories: one category for words, one for sounds and one that explains the meaning of the group of signs immediately preceding them— but we can still have fun by doing a simple form of Egyptian writing (try your own name, perhaps) using this **basic hieroglyphic alphabet.** 👉

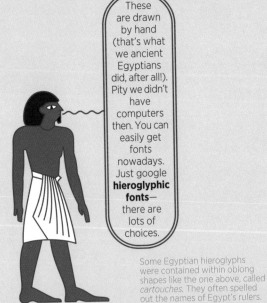

These are drawn by hand (that's what we ancient Egyptians did, after all!). Pity we didn't have computers then. You can easily get fonts nowadays. Just google **hieroglyphic fonts**— there are lots of choices.

Some Egyptian hieroglyphs were contained within oblong shapes like the one above, called *cartouches.* They often spelled out the names of Egypt's rulers.

A Vulture

B Foot
(Some say this also stands for V.)

C Basket

D Hand

E Flowering reed

F Horned viper

G Jar stand

H House (floor plan)

I Flowering reed

J Cobra

K Basket

L Lion

M Owl

N Water

O Lasso

P Seat

Q Hill

R Mouth

S Folded cloth

T Egyptian bread loaf

U, W Quail chick

X Basket and cloth

Y Two flowering reeds

Z Door bolt

Who's happy, who's not?

The World Happiness Report was first released in April 2012, in support of the UN's "Wellbeing and Happiness" meeting. Here's the ranking of all 156 countries in the 7th Report, released in 2019, from happiest at the left to least happy down there.

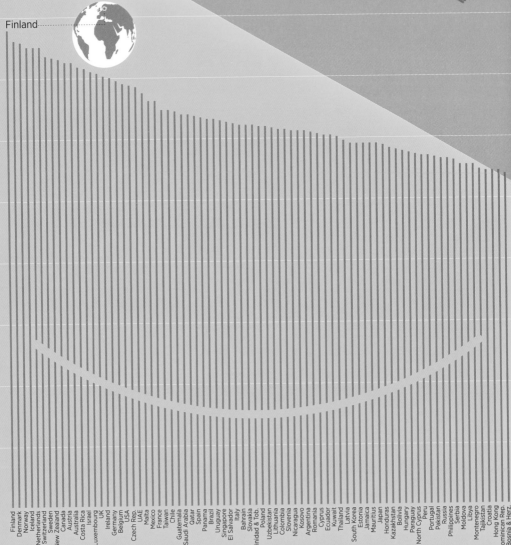

Finland

Finland
Denmark
Norway
Iceland
Netherlands
Switzerland
Sweden
New Zealand
Canada
Austria
Australia
Costa Rica
Israel
Luxembourg
UK
Ireland
Germany
Belgium
USA
Czech Rep.
UAE
Malta
Mexico
France
Taiwan
Chile
Guatemala
Saudi Arabia
Qatar
Spain
Panama
Brazil
Uruguay
Singapore
El Salvador
Italy
Bahrain
Slovakia
Trinidad & Tob.
Poland
Uzbekistan
Lithuania
Colombia
Slovenia
Nicaragua
Kosovo
Argentina
Romania
Cyprus
Ecuador
Kuwait
Thailand
Latvia
South Korea
Estonia
Jamaica
Mauritius
Japan
Honduras
Kazakhstan
Bolivia
Hungary
Paraguay
Peru
North Cyprus
Portugal
Pakistan
Russia
Philippines
Serbia
Moldova
Libya
Montenegro
Tajikistan
Croatia
Hong Kong
Dominican Rep.
Bosnia & Herz.

The list was compiled by averaging a number of factors, each scored from 0–10, including **GDP per capita, perceptions of corruption, social support, healthy life expectancy, freedom to make choices, and generosity.** Unlike previous happiness lists, these rankings are not connected solely to income.

Bhutan's Gross National Happiness (GNH) index is an inspiration for the UN list. Formalised in 2010, the GNH aims at the goal of happiness over the goal of wealth. But this was not a new thing for that country. The Bhutanese legal code of 1729 stated: **"If the Government cannot create happiness for its people, there is no purpose for the Government to exist."** Nice!

Bhutan
is ranked 95th
out of the
156 countries.

8

7

6

5

4

3
South
Sudan

2

1

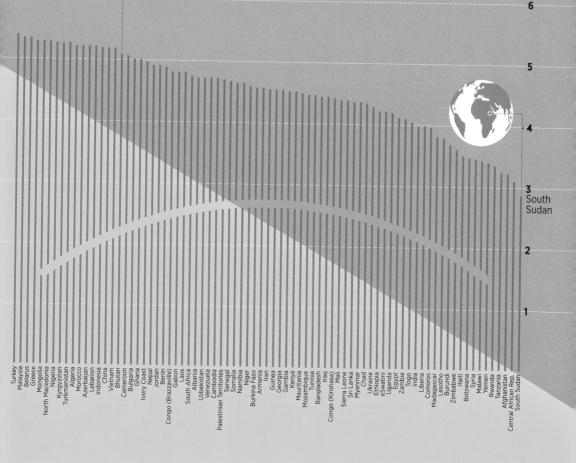

Turkey
Malaysia
Belarus
Greece
Mongolia
North Macedonia
Nigeria
Kyrgyzstan
Turkmenistan
Algeria
Morocco
Azerbaijan
Lebanon
Indonesia
China
Vietnam
Bhutan
Cameroon
Bulgaria
Ghana
Ivory Coast
Nepal
Jordan
Benin
Congo (Brazzaville)
Gabon
Laos
South Africa
Albania
Uzbekistan
Venezuela
Cambodia
Palestinian Territories
Senegal
Somalia
Namibia
Niger
Burkina Faso
Armenia
Iran
Guinea
Georgia
Gambia
Kenya
Mauritania
Mozambique
Tunisia
Bangladesh
Iraq
Congo (Kinshasa)
Mali
Sierra Leone
Sri Lanka
Myanmar
Chad
Ukraine
Ethiopia
eSwatini
Uganda
Egypt
Zambia
Togo
India
Liberia
Comoros
Madagascar
Lesotho
Burundi
Zimbabwe
Haiti
Botswana
Syria
Malawi
Yemen
Rwanda
Tanzania
Afghanistan
Central African Rep.
South Sudan

Disappearing diversity

There are over 5000 indigenous groups in the world. They represent many ways that humans have adapted to almost every environment.

But most of these people are facing a variety of threats including **deforestation, disease, legal and illegal resource exploitation, climate change, the loss of traditional languages, and being removed from their homelands.** Some of the most at-risk groups shown here may not be around for much longer.

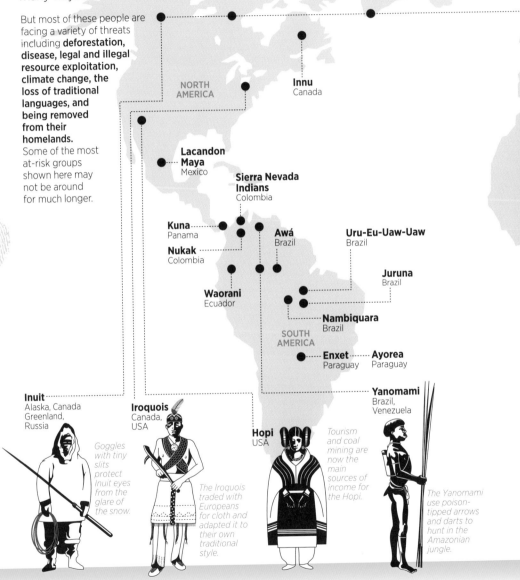

NORTH AMERICA

Innu
Canada

Lacandon Maya
Mexico

Sierra Nevada Indians
Colombia

Kuna
Panama

Nukak
Colombia

Awá
Brazil

Uru-Eu-Uaw-Uaw
Brazil

Juruna
Brazil

Waorani
Ecuador

Nambiquara
Brazil

SOUTH AMERICA

Enxet
Paraguay

Ayorea
Paraguay

Yanomami
Brazil, Venezuela

Inuit
Alaska, Canada Greenland, Russia

Goggles with tiny slits protect Inuit eyes from the glare of the snow.

Iroquois
Canada, USA

The Iroquois traded with Europeans for cloth and adapted it to their own traditional style.

Hopi
USA

Tourism and coal mining are now the main sources of income for the Hopi.

The Yanomami use poison-tipped arrows and darts to hunt in the Amazonian jungle.

Sami
Northern
Scandinavia

Nenets
North Western Siberia

Livonians
Latvia

ASIA

Akha
China,
Myanmar
(Burma),
Thailand

EUROPE

Dukha
Northern
Mongolia

Ainu
Japan, Russia

Yazidi
Northern
Iraq

**Dongria
Kondh**
India

Jumma
Bangladesh

Batak
Philippines

AFRICA

Palawan
Philippines

Vedda
Sri Lanka

Onge
India
(Andaman
Islands)

S'aoch
Cambodia

Yali
Indonesia

El Molo
Kenya

Penan
Borneo

Ogiek
Kenya

Jarawa
India
(Andaman
Islands)

Mentawai
Indonesia

Hupla
Indonesia

**Aboriginal
People**
Australia

OCEANIA

Bushmen
Southern
Africa

Pygmies
Central
Africa

Nuba
South
Sudan

Tuareg
Sahara

*Long blue
veils shade
the Tuareg
from the
desert sun.*

*Bushmen
survive by
hunting wild
animals and
gathering plants.*

*Many
forest-dwelling
Pygmies are
still living as
hunter-gatherers.*

*The Nuba must
carry water to the
family home every
day in order to survive.*

How to predict the weather from the clouds

Long before the digital "cloud", there was the weather forecasting cloud. But do we ever believe the weather forecast? That science is more complicated than just looking at the clouds, of course, but this guide might just help you plan that picnic next weekend.

metres
12,200

What the names mean

Cirrus Curl (as of hair)
Stratus Layer, spread over an area
Cumulus Heap of clouds
Nimbus Rain-bearing

Cirrostratus
Rain in the next
12–24 hours

9,150

Cirrocumulus
Fair weather
(In the tropics,
this cloud can
mean a storm
is approaching.)

Altocumulus
Possibility
of thunder

7,000

Nimbostratus
Rain

3,050

Stratus
(This cloud looks
like elevated fog.)
Drizzle,
light snow

Cumulonimbus
(Cumulus clouds that have grown
into the classic anvil shape.)
Rain, thunder, lightning, hail,
flash floods, tornadoes

feet
40,000

Cirrus
Fair weather

30,000

Cruising altitude of jet airliners

The phrase "cloud nine" is
said to have originated
with the US Weather Bureau,
which once classified clouds by
number. Cumulonimbus was
number nine on the list, since
it's the cloud that climbs
farthest into the sky. So if you're
on cloud nine, you're happily
on top of the world.*

*A little scepticism
is in order.
1. There are
generally
considered to be
ten distinct cloud
formations.
2. This might be the
tallest cloud, but it's
not the happiest!

20,000

Altostratus
Rain in the next
12–24 hours

Cumulus
Fair weather

Stratocumulus
Generally means
dry weather

10,000

Snow joke

Before it all disappears
in a warming world,
**here's a look at how
snow is formed
and then changes
as it falls to Earth.**

1

Between 11 and 13
kilometres (7–8
miles) above the
earth, water vapour
condenses and
becomes liquid.

2

The droplets grow
and form ice
crystals around
minute particles
floating in the
atmosphere.

Pollen
or dust
particle

Look at all these
Inuit words
for snow!*

MAUJA
(deep, soft snow)

UPSIK
(compacted snow)

APUN
(snow on the ground)

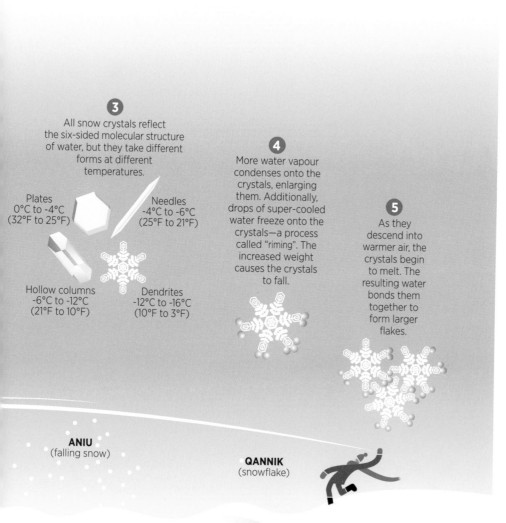

3
All snow crystals reflect the six-sided molecular structure of water, but they take different forms at different temperatures.

Plates
0°C to -4°C
(32°F to 25°F)

Needles
-4°C to -6°C
(25°F to 21°F)

Hollow columns
-6°C to -12°C
(21°F to 10°F)

Dendrites
-12°C to -16°C
(10°F to 3°F)

4
More water vapour condenses onto the crystals, enlarging them. Additionally, drops of super-cooled water freeze onto the crystals—a process called "riming". The increased weight causes the crystals to fall.

5
As they descend into warmer air, the crystals begin to melt. The resulting water bonds them together to form larger flakes.

ANIU
(falling snow)

QANNIK
(snowflake)

*It's a myth that Inuits have hundreds of words for snow. The ones above are about it.

The **Sami**, however, *do* have very many names for the quality, depth and what-animal-has-just-been-on-it snow. The Sami are an Arctic indigenous people who live in the far north of Sweden, Norway, Finland and Russia.

The world's electrical outlets

Most countries use one or more of these 13 shapes.
(A selection of representative countries are listed.)
Make sure your appliances have the right plugs or adaptors.

Type A   Type B

Antigua and Barbuda,
Bahamas, Barbados,
Belize, Bermuda,
Canada, Colombia,
Costa Rica, Cuba,
Ecuador, Guatemala,
Honduras, Jamaica,
Japan, Mexico, Panama,
Peru, Puerto Rico, Saudi
Arabia, Tahiti, Thailand,
USA, Venezuela

Type C

Afghanistan, Albania, Algeria, Angola,
Argentina, Armenia, Austria, Belgium,
Benin, Bolivia, Bosnia and Herzegovina,
Brazil, Bulgaria, Cambodia, Chile, China,
Croatia, Czech Republic, Denmark, Egypt,
Ethiopia, Finland, France, Gabon,
Germany, Greece, Hungary, Iceland, India,
Indonesia, Iran, Iraq, Israel, Italy, Kuwait,
Libya, Macedonia, Malaysia, Mongolia,
Morocco, Mozambique, Nepal,
Netherlands, Norway, Pakistan, Peru,
Poland, Portugal, Russia, Serbia,
Singapore, Somalia, South Africa, South
Korea, Spain, Sudan, Sweden, Syria,
Thailand, Tunisia, Turkey, Ukraine, Zambia

Type D

Ethiopia, Ghana,
Greece, Hong
Kong, India, Iraq,
Kuwait, Libya,
Nepal, Nigeria,
Pakistan, South
Africa, Sudan,
Zambia, Zimbabwe

Type H

Gaza,
Israel

Type I

Argentina,
Australia, China,
Fiji, New
Zealand, Samoa

Type J

Switzerland

Type E

Belgium, Benin, Cambodia, Czech Republic, Denmark, Ethiopia, France, Greece, Madagascar, Mongolia, Morocco, Poland, Slovakia, Spain, Syria, Tahiti, Tunisia

Type F

Afghanistan, Albania, Algeria, Armenia, Austria, Bosnia and Herzegovina, Bulgaria, Croatia, Denmark, Egypt, Ethiopia, Finland, Germany, Greece, Hungary, Iceland, Indonesia, Iran, Italy, Libya, Macedonia, Mozambique, Netherlands, Norway, Portugal, Russia, Saudi Arabia, Serbia, South Korea, Spain, Sweden, Thailand, Turkey, Ukraine

Type G

Bahrain, Belize, Cambodia, Channel Islands, China, Cyprus, Ghana, Guatemala, Hong Kong, Indonesia, Iraq, Ireland, Kenya, Kuwait, Malawi, Malaysia, Malta, Nigeria, Pakistan, Saudi Arabia, Seychelles, Singapore, St Lucia, Uganda, UK, Zambia, Zimbabwe

Type K

Denmark

Type L

Chile, Ethiopia, Italy, Libya, Spain, Syria

Type M

Botswana, India, Israel, Kuwait, Malaysia, Mozambique, Namibia, Pakistan, Singapore, South Africa

The difference between an Interpreter ... and a ... translator

deals with the
spoken
word

deals with the
written
word

The **interpreter** is present
at an event and conveys the speaker's words
to an audience in a different language.
The interpreter must decide on the spot
what words best convey the meaning.

Je ne sais quoi

literally ⟶ *I do not know*

common usage

Interpreter
decides to leave it
in the French
for the audience
to hear

That certain something that can't be defined

Je ne sais quoi

Interpreters work in two ways:

Simultaneous

Used at conferences and major political speeches
(such as at the United Nations). The interpreter is in a sound-proof
booth speaking into a microphone and the audience has earphones
so that all they hear are the interpreter's words in their own language.

Consecutive

Here the interpreter is generally
standing next to or near the speaker, who delivers one or two sentences,
and then shuts up (the interpreter hopes!) to allow the interpreter
to convey the meaning.

Interpreters (on phones) are employed in stores or hospitals
where a shopper or patient doesn't know the language and needs help.
It's a much cheaper, although much less personal, alternative to having
a person walking around helping people.

The **translator** is seldom present
when a writer is writing.

So, unlike interpreting, translation is used where anything written,
for instance, business and legal documents, can be read by someone
who doesn't know the language.

Also unlike an interpreter, a translator can make extensive use of
computer programs in the preparation of a translated text.
The main constraint is the deadline!

An important aspect of the job is the translation of non-fiction and fiction —
in some cases, the great works of literature.

When it went wrong ... or did it?

Don't believe the "I am a doughnut" story!

A popular case of misinterpretation involved John F. Kennedy's
famous speech in Berlin on June 26th, 1963, when he expressed solidarity
with the people of West Berlin by declaring
"Ich bin ein Berliner!"
In parts of Germany, Berliner means jelly doughnut,
and in the years that followed the speech the idea grew that
the president had declared himself to be a pastry.
In fact his grammar was tip-top, but it's such a delicious story,
it won't go away!

OUTDOORS

Alligators and crocodiles: precautions ...

1 Sounds obvious, but **don't swim** (or dangle your arm off a boat) in lakes and rivers that locals warn you might have crocs or gators in them.

2 If you see one, **stay at least 4.5m (15ft) away.** In the water they can swim much faster than you; on land, they can move surprisingly quickly, so ...

3 On land, **run** in a straight line away from the water. They will pursue you moving very fast, but only for a short time, before tiring and giving up.

The tail provides the main thrust when swimming ...

and back claws are webbed to give extra propulsion in the water.

That's why they can swim faster than you. Don't try to find out if it's true!

and defensive measures

**OK, so you tried to get out of the way,
but one of them catches you. Here's what to do:**

4 **Poke the eyes** with a stick, or anything you have. Their eyes are their most vulnerable part.

5 **Strike the nostrils and ears hard,** with your fist or a heavy stick.

The ears (↓) are just behind the eyes, hard to see. There are movable flaps over them that stop water from going in.

The nostrils are on top of the snout so that the rest of the body can be submerged, out of sight.

6 If your arm or leg is inside the mouth, you might be able to **push the palatal valve down to the tongue.** 🖝 Water will flow in, and the animal will let you go.

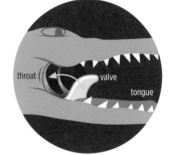

throat   valve   tongue

The palatal valve is a flap of tissue behind the tongue that swings back to close off the throat and prevent drowning when the mouth is open.

Teeth are not used for chewing; they grab and hold prey—you! (Although you're by no means their main prey, which is usually swallowed whole.)

How to survive (and prevent) a shark attack

Keep your fears in proportion; you are more likely to be hurt by overexposure to the sun than you are to be bitten by a shark.

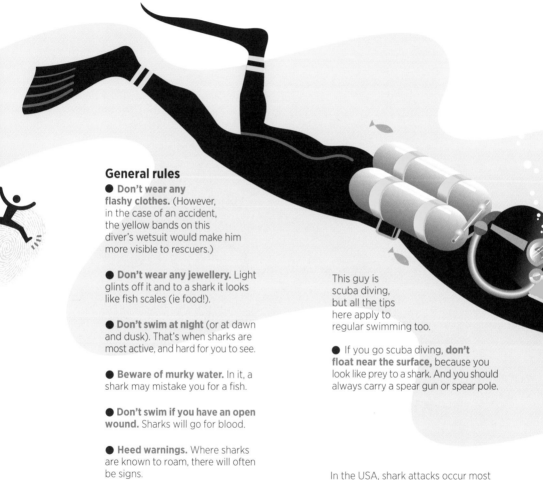

General rules

● **Don't wear any flashy clothes.** (However, in the case of an accident, the yellow bands on this diver's wetsuit would make him more visible to rescuers.)

● **Don't wear any jewellery.** Light glints off it and to a shark it looks like fish scales (ie food!).

● **Don't swim at night** (or at dawn and dusk). That's when sharks are most active, and hard for you to see.

● **Beware of murky water.** In it, a shark may mistake you for a fish.

● **Don't swim if you have an open wound.** Sharks will go for blood.

● **Heed warnings.** Where sharks are known to roam, there will often be signs.

● **Stay away from deep drop-offs underwater.** This is where sharks like to congregate.

This guy is scuba diving, but all the tips here apply to regular swimming too.

● If you go scuba diving, **don't float near the surface,** because you look like prey to a shark. And you should always carry a spear gun or spear pole.

In the USA, shark attacks occur most frequently in waters off Florida, but the California coast and all around Hawaii are also dangerous, as well as waters around Australia and South Africa.

Basic self-defence

● **Stay in groups while you swim.**
Sharks are less likely to attack
a group of swimmers than
an individual.

● **If a shark approaches you,** use
anything you have to strike at it—
your camera, for instance, or your
fist or a spear gun.

● **Don't go for the nose:**
a shark's eyes and gills are the most
sensitive and painful areas to hit.

THE THREE MOST DANGEROUS SHARKS (average lengths)

GREAT WHITE 4.5m (15ft)   **TIGER** 3m (10ft)   **BULL** 2m (7ft)

How to avoid being sucked into quicksand ...

It's usually found near coasts and inland on riverbanks or near lakes, marshes and underground springs.

1 If you are walking in an area known to have quicksands, carry a **strong pole** with you.

2 If you feel yourself sinking, put the pole on the ground in front of you.

3 With the pole perpendicular to your body, lie across the pole.

4 Don't panic. The more you wiggle around, the faster you will sink. But **you will never sink completely,** because your body is not as dense as the surrounding sand. (You know you can float on water, and sand is denser than water; so it's easier to float in quicksand than on water.) **If you don't have a pole, don't worry, you'll still float.**

In general, quicksand is not that deep. The problem is the vacuum that's formed when you try to lift your legs once they are in the sand— jerky movements will suck you in further.

5 Spread your arms out to increase your surface area. Lie back and relax. With gentle movements, slowly work yourself to a safe area.

(I know, easier said than done!)

Quicksands are often depicted in movies as deadly: in real life they are not.

but if you can't, this is what's happening under you

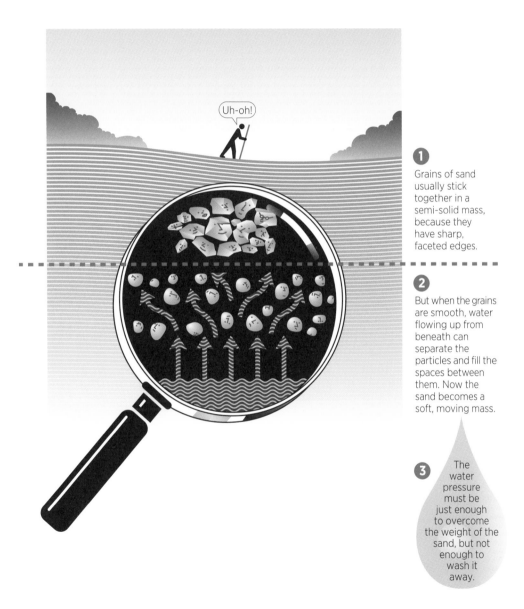

1 Grains of sand usually stick together in a semi-solid mass, because they have sharp, faceted edges.

2 But when the grains are smooth, water flowing up from beneath can separate the particles and fill the spaces between them. Now the sand becomes a soft, moving mass.

3 The water pressure must be just enough to overcome the weight of the sand, but not enough to wash it away.

How to stop mosquitoes from fuelling up ... on you

(Spanish for "little fly")

THEY'LL DRINK YOUR BLOOD ...

Hidden inside the mosquito's proboscis are six "stylets" (hypodermic-like needles) that penetrate just far enough under the skin to find a blood vessel*.

Mnnnnmmm! This'll do nicely for a few days!

Males live from 5 to 7 days; females from 2 weeks to a month.

Proboscis

*A second tube inside the proboscis injects **saliva** into the bite area, and this causes the swelling and itching.

Mosquitoes can **smell** human breath (the carbon dioxide we exhale) from around 100m (328ft) away.

Anopheles mosquitoes spread **malaria** by drinking the blood of an infected person and then biting another. Aedes aegypti mosquitoes carry **dengue fever.**

A female mosquito can drink between 0.001mL and 0.01mL of blood before her abdomen is full (females bite, males don't).

It would take about 1.2 million bites to drain all your blood.

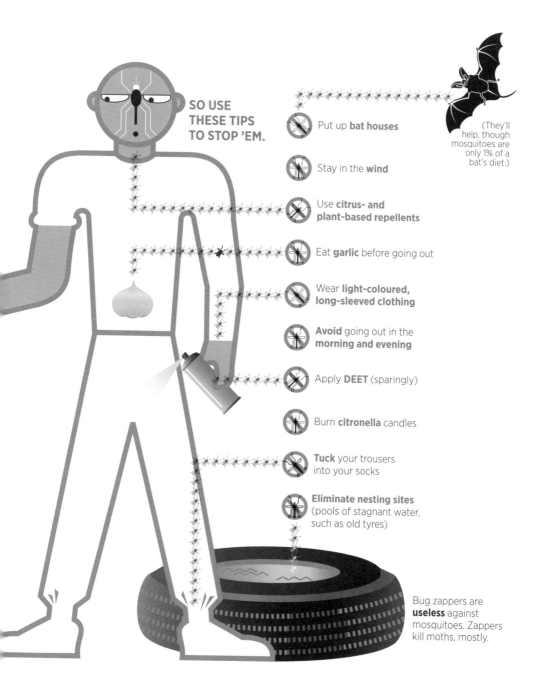

SO USE THESE TIPS TO STOP 'EM.

Put up **bat houses**

(They'll help, though mosquitoes are only 1% of a bat's diet.)

Stay in the **wind**

Use **citrus- and plant-based repellents**

Eat **garlic** before going out

Wear **light-coloured, long-sleeved clothing**

Avoid going out in the **morning and evening**

Apply **DEET** (sparingly)

Burn **citronella** candles

Tuck your trousers into your socks

Eliminate nesting sites (pools of stagnant water, such as old tyres)

Bug zappers are **useless** against mosquitoes. Zappers kill moths, mostly.

Recognising animal tracks

See who's been walking around. Africa, this page, and North America, opposite.

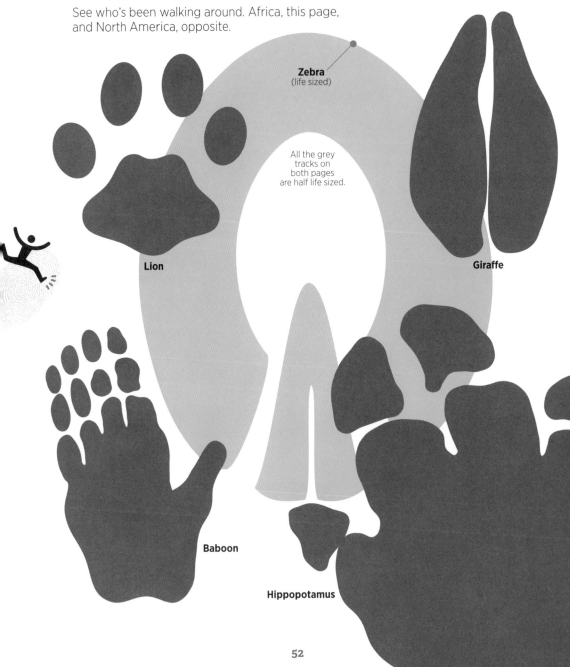

Zebra
(life sized)

All the grey tracks on both pages are half life sized.

Lion

Giraffe

Baboon

Hippopotamus

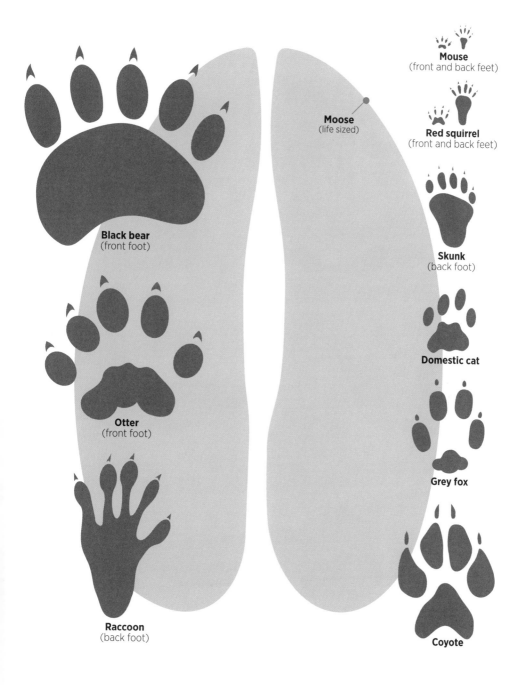

Moose
(life sized)

Mouse
(front and back feet)

Red squirrel
(front and back feet)

Skunk
(back foot)

Domestic cat

Grey fox

Coyote

Black bear
(front foot)

Otter
(front foot)

Raccoon
(back foot)

Recognising animal poop

Smart hikers call it **scat.** All these are drawn **life sized.**

Mouse Their scat is found near their nests, and can take lots of different irregular shapes.

Red squirrel This scat is very similar to that of the grey squirrel, but while red squirrels prefer a coniferous habitat, greys prefer a deciduous one, so where you find it is the best way to tell their poop apart.

Beaver The poop is composed of wood chips, but it's almost never seen because beavers spend most of their time in water, where the poop decomposes.

Weasel The scat is twisted into a long cylinder, and contains hair and bone splinters.

Porcupine You'll see bark, twigs and tree buds in porcupoop. It has a strong smell of urine. The scat may be found as separate pellets or in a chain linked by wood fibres.

Moose The droppings mostly consist of twigs (red maple is a favourite). In winter, the scat is composed of separate blobs; in summer it looks more like a cow pat.

Red fox The poop contains hair, bones, insects and berry seeds. It's often found on a rock or stump, marking the animal's territory.

Coyote The colour of this scat varies according to the animal's diet, but it usually contains hair, bones and berries.

Black bear The scat contains remnants of animals, nuts, berries, grasses, insects and fish. Bears are omnivorous, and it shows!

African lion Most of what shows in lion scat is fur. This might be from any number of animals, including buffalo, impala, warthogs, wildebeest and zebras.

And what about us humans?
What is the correct outdoor pooping etiquette?
If you are on a camping holiday with friends, **decide on a plan.** There'll be giggles, but you do need some rules.

1 No pooping nearer to camp than 50m (165ft).

2 On a tree branch near the camp, hang a bag containing toilet paper and a small spade. (Then, if the bag is missing, someone is using the woods!)

3 Use the spade to dig a "cat-hole"—just remove about 5cm (2in) of topsoil.

4 When you are done, cover up the poop with a mound of soil, the way a cat does in its litter box. Poop will compost sooner in a shallow trench like this than it will in a deep hole.

5 If you have a strong campfire going, burn your used toilet paper. If not, bury it with the poop. (Maple or other flat leaves are a good substitute loo paper.)

A tall story to tell round the fire
In the Middle Ages, **manure** was a major trading commodity. But it was heavy, due to all the moisture in it, so exporters dried the manure out before loading it onto the wooden ships of the day. In rough seas, water came in through portholes in the cargo holds and this action started the process of **methane production** in the manure. If an unsuspecting seaman went below deck for a quick smoke ... **BOOM!!**

So to protect against this, the bales of dried manure were labelled **Store High In Transit** (in other words, on deck in the open air). The stuff still got wet, but the sun dried it off.

Store **H**igh **I**n **T**ransit was soon shortened to its initial letters.

Lost in the desert? Here's what to do

If you are in a car, ask yourself these questions:

Will anyone miss me?
Will they try to come and find me?
Will they notify emergency help or anyone else?

If you said **YES**   If you said **NO**

1
Stay where you are, in the car.

2
Signal for help.
The international ground-to-air distress signal is material (anything you can find) arranged in a large V-shape on the ground. At night, if you can, build a number of small fires in this shape.

Another more impressive, but riskier, signal is the tree torch. You must be careful to select a tree that stands alone in an open space.

1
Get moving at night—
this will help you save energy, and avoid heat and dehydration.

2
Orient yourself.
The night sky is your guide.

Note: this will only work for those in the Northern Hemisphere.

3
Now you know which direction is which, **consult your map.**
You do have a map, right?

An improvised shelter
(This will protect you from sandstorms and the sun.)

Leaves or clothing draped over a twig frame.

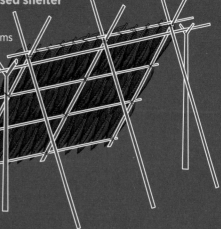

the Big Dipper
(Ursa Major)

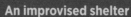

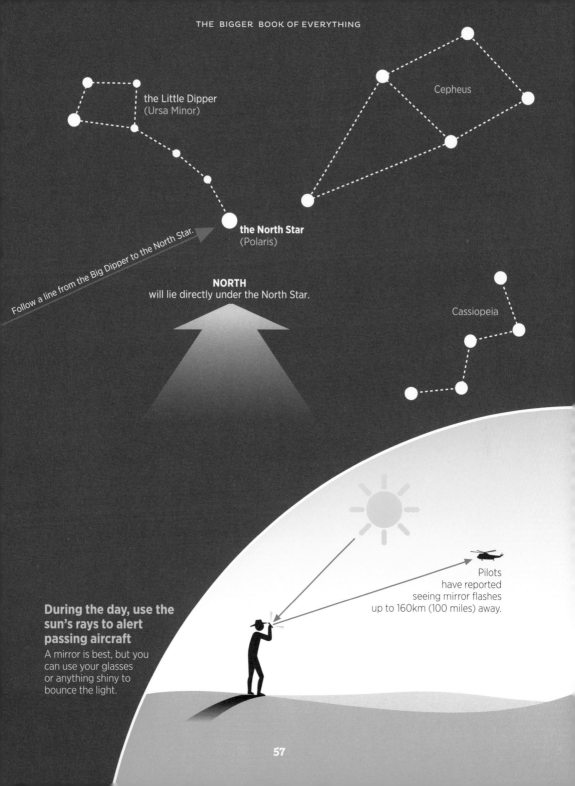

the Little Dipper
(Ursa Minor)

Cepheus

Follow a line from the Big Dipper to the North Star.

the North Star
(Polaris)

NORTH
will lie directly under the North Star.

Cassiopeia

Pilots
have reported
seeing mirror flashes
up to 160km (100 miles) away.

**During the day, use the
sun's rays to alert
passing aircraft**
A mirror is best, but you
can use your glasses
or anything shiny to
bounce the light.

Lost on a hike: six stages of survival

Psychologists call it "woods shock", and they can predict how you will act when it happens to you. Here are the downs and ups of survival in the wild.

Disorientation
Which is the right way to go?

Urgency
The impulse to run

Panic
Stumbling, and throwing gear away

Most people keep going forward; few turn round and go back. Returning to the last known place would probably be the best thing for you to do, but at this stage, your denial that anything is really wrong is particularly influential.

With your surroundings seeming to close in around you, you may try to "break out" from the situation and start running.

Thinking that lightening your load will result in extra speed, you'll more than likely discard backpacks, food and other equipment.

If you can find a clear area ...

These are the internationally recognised **ground-to-air signals.** Make them with strips of clothing, foliage—anything you can find that contrasts with the ground. And **make them big** so they can be seen from the air.

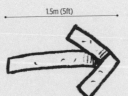

1.5m (5ft)

I AM MOVING IN THIS DIRECTION

NEED DOCTOR — SERIOUS INJURY

NEED MEDICAL SUPPLIES

④ Planning
Trying to think of
the way back

⑤ Fatigue
Loss of will
to live

⑥ Optimism
Determination and
a sense of humour

Having survived
the initial burst of panic,
some people try to
form a logical plan of
escape. But usually you
are too tired, and by
now are a long way
away from your original
track, so your plans
usually fail.

The lowest point.
When your plan fails,
you'll be emotionally
and physically drained.
You'll finally admit you
are lost and stop
making any moves to
help yourself, such as
building a shelter
or fire.

The will to live depends
less on equipment (the materials
to make a fire, for instance) than
it does on mental strength.
Thinking about seeing family
and friends again instead of
dwelling on the apparent
hopelessness of the situation
will often pull you through. Try
to keep a sense of humour. Set
small goals; finish them. Build a
shelter. Stay busy. You know
others are looking for you.

NEED FOOD
AND WATER

PROBABLY SAFE
TO LAND HERE

IF IN DOUBT, USE THIS
INTERNATIONAL SYMBOL

Camping tips

Respect for nature
and common sense
are the hallmarks
of good camping.
Follow these simple
rules for a safer and
more enjoyable
outdoor trip.

①
**MOST
IMPORTANT:**
Select your
site **before
daylight
fades.**

②
The best protection
against lightning
is a **stand of
medium-sized trees.**

③
**Set up your kitchen at least 60m
(200ft) downwind** from your tent. This
will make sure that the remnants of
anything edible or fragrant are far away
from you at night (bears' supper time).

To prevent pollution,
**keep the fire or
stove well away
from water
sources.**

A small stove
will do far less
harm to the
environment
than a fire.

④
Choose a **flat,
well-drained site** for
the tent. If the soil is
compressed or soggy,
it will not drain well
in case of rain.

**Never dig a trench
to divert water.**
If there's a slope to
the floor of the tent,
make sure you sleep
with your head higher
than your feet.

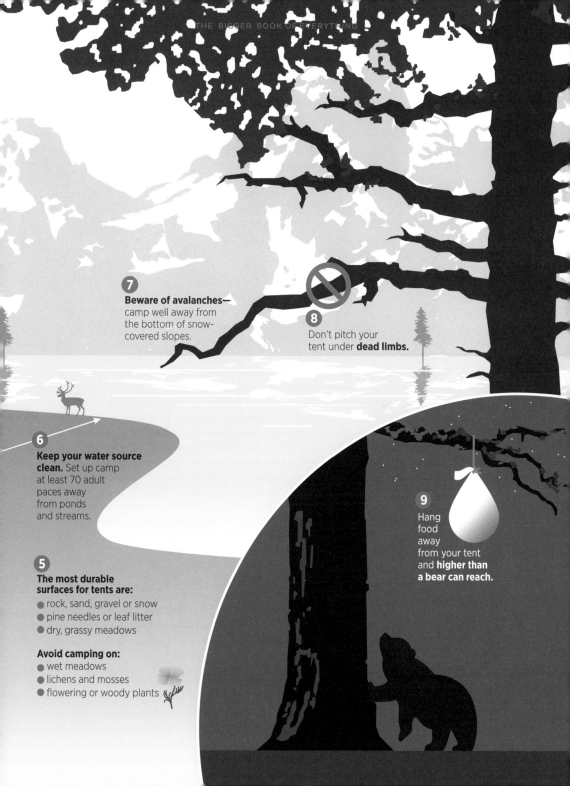

7 Beware of avalanches—camp well away from the bottom of snow-covered slopes.

8 Don't pitch your tent under **dead limbs.**

6 **Keep your water source clean.** Set up camp at least 70 adult paces away from ponds and streams.

9 Hang food away from your tent and **higher than a bear can reach.**

5 **The most durable surfaces for tents are:**
- rock, sand, gravel or snow
- pine needles or leaf litter
- dry, grassy meadows

Avoid camping on:
- wet meadows
- lichens and mosses
- flowering or woody plants

The rules of the campfire

Most important: leave the site the way you found it.

1

Finding fuel
Gather more dry stuff
than you think you'll need.
You can always put it back
where you found it.

The main
pieces of wood
should be the
length of your
forearm and
about as wide
as the diameter
of your wrist.

Sticks for **kindling**
should be the
thickness of a pencil.

Tinder (twigs, dried
grass or shredded
dry leaves) should
be toothpick-sized.

2

Building the fire
Choose a site on
exposed bedrock,
grass or scattered
leaves.

OXYGEN FLOW

Place a
tarp that's
1m (39in)
square at
least 3m
(10ft) away
from dry
grass.

**Mineral
soil**
12cm
(5in) high,
insulates
ground
and tarp
from heat.

Build a
"teepee"
by lodging
wood
in the
mineral
soil.

An **opening**
allows you to
insert tinder
and kindling.

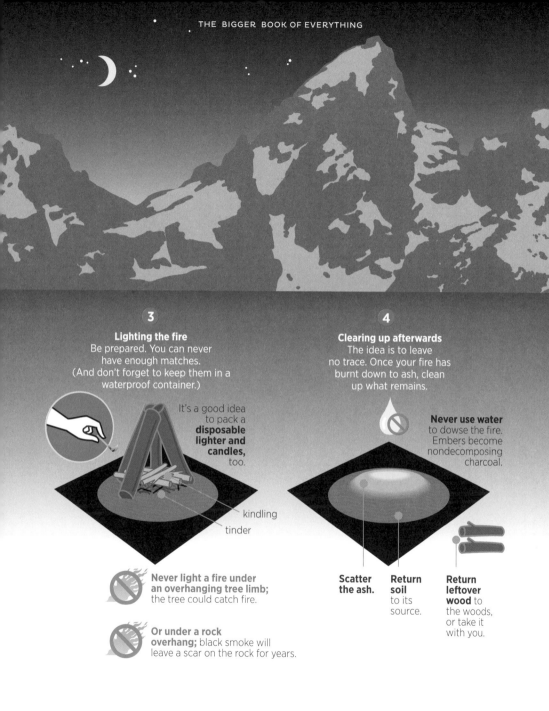

3

Lighting the fire
Be prepared. You can never have enough matches. (And don't forget to keep them in a waterproof container.)

It's a good idea to pack a **disposable lighter and candles,** too.

kindling

tinder

Never light a fire under an overhanging tree limb; the tree could catch fire.

Or under a rock overhang; black smoke will leave a scar on the rock for years.

4

Clearing up afterwards
The idea is to leave no trace. Once your fire has burnt down to ash, clean up what remains.

Never use water to dowse the fire. Embers become nondecomposing charcoal.

Scatter the ash.

Return soil to its source.

Return leftover wood to the woods, or take it with you.

Staying warm and dry outdoors

High-tech fabrics, worn by themselves or in **layers,** provide a system for outdoor protection and comfort.

2 Middle layer
for warmth and insulation.

1 Base layer
for dryness.

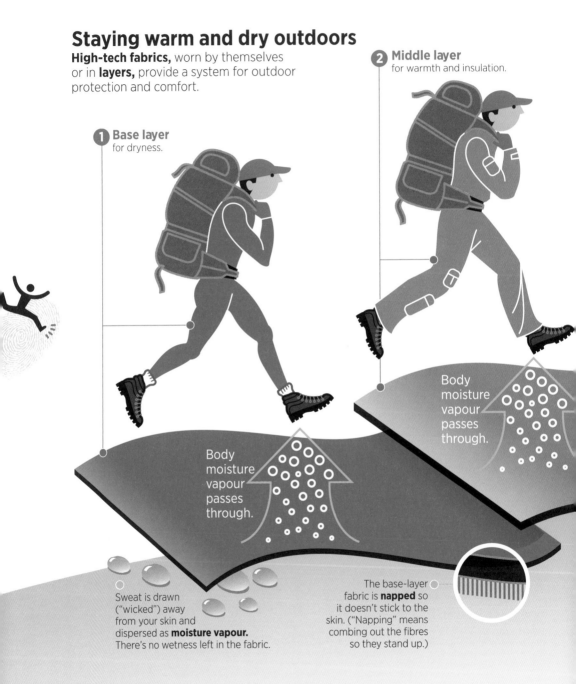

Body moisture vapour passes through.

Body moisture vapour passes through.

Sweat is drawn ("wicked") away from your skin and dispersed as **moisture vapour.** There's no wetness left in the fabric.

The base-layer fabric is **napped** so it doesn't stick to the skin. ("Napping" means combing out the fibres so they stand up.)

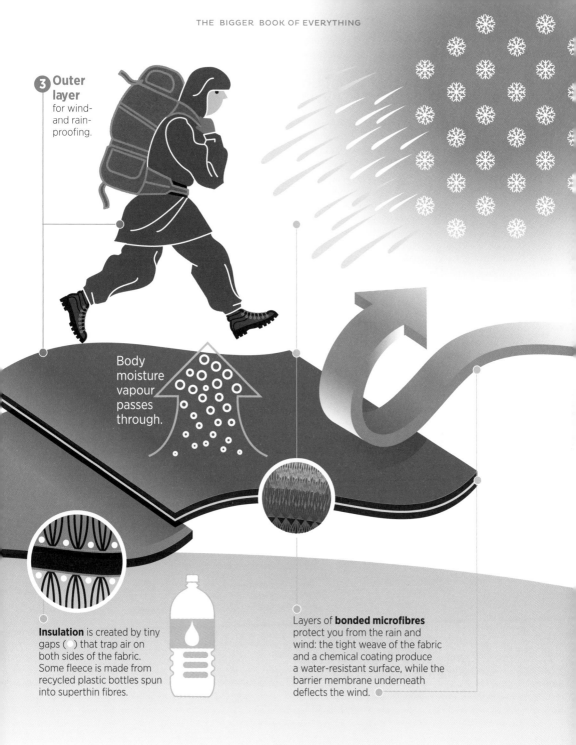

3 Outer layer for wind- and rain-proofing.

Body moisture vapour passes through.

Insulation is created by tiny gaps ( ) that trap air on both sides of the fabric. Some fleece is made from recycled plastic bottles spun into superthin fibres.

Layers of **bonded microfibres** protect you from the rain and wind: the tight weave of the fabric and a chemical coating produce a water-resistant surface, while the barrier membrane underneath deflects the wind.

How to get out of a sinking car

①

As soon as you realise that you are in water, **open the window.** This will allow water to flow into the car, making the pressure inside the car the same as outside. With equal pressure inside and out, you'll be able to open the door. Your car might float for a short time, but don't count on it.

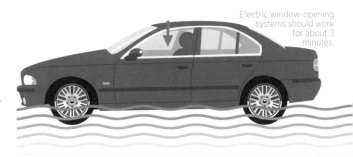

Electric window-opening systems should work for about 3 minutes.

②

If the most of the door is above the water level, you might be able to open it, but if not, **leave the door alone.** (You'll only have seconds before outside water pressure means that you can't open it anyway.)
Don't try to to use your mobile phone.
You do not have time.

③

Unbuckle your seat belt. Leaving a seat belt on might give you leverage when it's time to open the door (see **⑥**), but experts seem to agree that it is more important to be able to move around without your seat belt restraining you.

④

If the car has a front-mounted engine, it will go down at a steep angle. If you cannot open the window, try to **break the glass with a heavy object.** If you have a hammer, a laptop, steering-wheel lock or even an umbrella, aim it at the centre of the glass. You could also try **kicking the window out,** by aiming your heel at the front of it. Don't bother trying to break the windscreen: it's made of unbreakable glass.

Take a deep breath and swim out through the broken window. It will be a struggle because you are swimming against a strong inflow of water.

If you have still failed to open the window, wait until the car has almost filled with water. As it rises up to your nose, **take a deep breath and hold your nose.** When the car is full, (total time will be 1–2 minutes), the water will be over your head, the pressure of water will be the same on the inside of the car as the outside, and you will be able to open the door.

If the water is more than about 4.5m (15ft) deep, your car might flip over. Of course, that will make it much harder to get out, and that's why **you must act quickly.**

Let's go for a (long) walk

Sure, you need a backpack, maps and a compass, a first aid kit and food and water. But if you can **carry less** you'll keep going much longer.

See what happens when you take a load off your back.

2.5kg
(5lb)

4.5kg
(10lb)

11.5kg
(25lb)

Uneven ground plays havoc with your legs, adding **pressure on your knees.** When you lighten the load you carry; your knees will thank you!

Reducing the load

Shop around on the web for lightweight gear
(representative weights shown here).

- Depending on its capacity, the **backpack** itself should be light. You can find
packs with enough room for a three-day hike starting around 0.5kg (15oz).

Some of the other items you'll be taking:
- sleeping bag 0.5kg (16oz) ● sleeping pad 0.25kg (9oz) ● shelter (tent) 0.18kg (6.3oz).
- rain gear 0.3kg (10oz) ● stove 0.06kg (2oz) ● fuel 0.2kg (7oz)

Take food out of the packaging it comes in,
and put it into plastic bags.

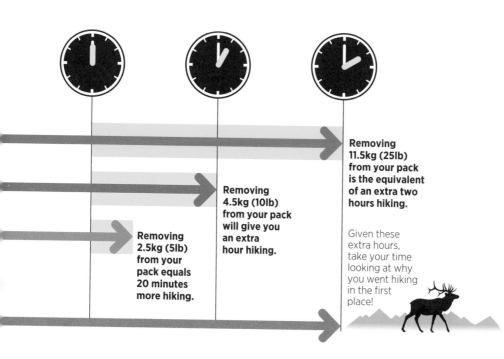

Removing
2.5kg (5lb)
from your
pack equals
20 minutes
more hiking.

Removing
4.5kg (10lb)
from your pack
will give you
an extra
hour hiking.

Removing
11.5kg (25lb)
from your pack
is the equivalent
of an extra two
hours hiking.

Given these
extra hours,
take your time
looking at why
you went hiking
in the first
place!

The birds you'll see depends on where you go

There are no parakeets in Paris, no penguins in Portugal, and no toucans in Tokyo*, but dedicated birdwatchers would go pretty much anywhere if they thought the trip would add another bird to their personal checklist of sightings.

Can you name these very different birds?

As a newly dedicated birdwatcher you'll have to do some travelling to see them for yourselves.

*As far as we know ... But, alright readers, tell us we're wrong, (Zoos and pets don't count.)

1. Northern Cardinal
2. California Condor
3. Scarlet Macaw
4. Toco Toucan
5. Yellow-tailed Black Cockatoo
6. Blue Tit
7. Secretary Bird
8. Red-throated Parrot Finch
9. Mandarin Duck

71

Watching birds

What's weird about this picture? The ears, right? But that's the point: your ears are almost as important as your eyes when you are birdwatching.

1 Learn bird sounds

Lots of apps let you hear different songs. Outdoors, these songs are your first clues to what birds might be in the area that you are watching.

2 Match illustrations to sounds

A good guidebook's pictures should also indicate the typical heights or locations that specific birds perch.

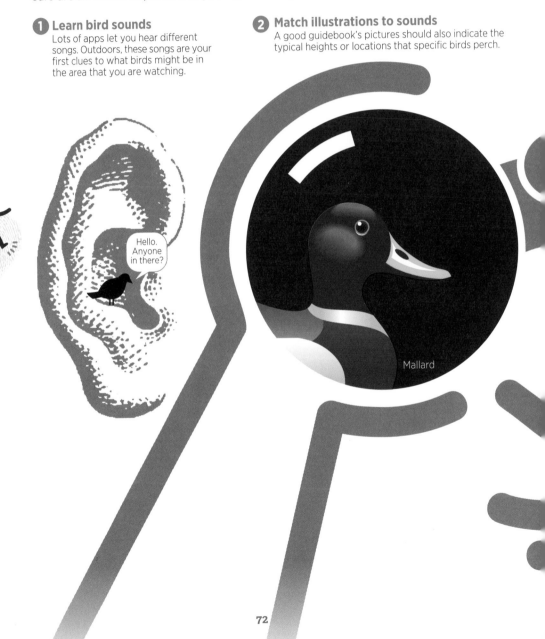

3 Now you know what you are looking for

Focus on where the sounds come from.
Up high? Eye level? On the ground?

4 No sounds?

Let's say you're indoors watching birds at the feeder. They can't sing and eat at the same time, silly! But do keep your guidebook near the window. This is often the best time to see birds for extended periods.

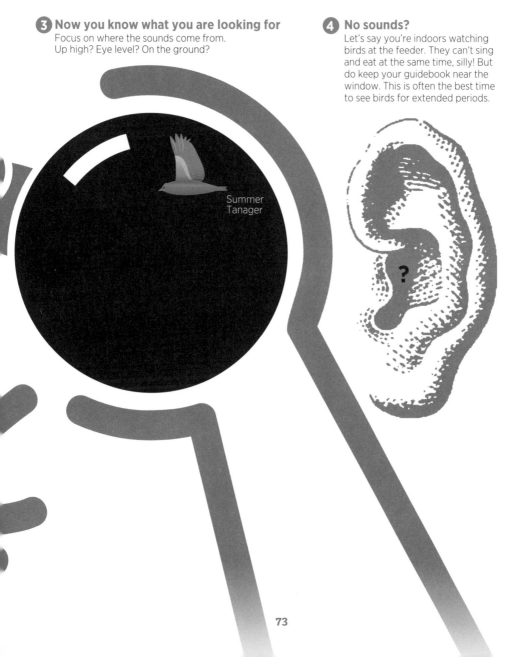

Summer
Tanager

Diving for pearls

Traditional pearl diving (*ama*) is 2000 years old. Originally, the divers were mostly women, who dove about 30m (100ft) without any breathing apparatus.

Today *ama* has been supplanted by cultured pearl farms. Some *ama* divers remain, but they work mostly in the tourist industry.

Ama: the old way

1 Holding onto a short rope (yellow) that's secured to the boat, the diver takes a deep breath.

2 A weighted rope (orange) helps the diver descend.

The third rope (green) is to help the ascent.

3 Near the bottom, the diver unhooks the weight-rope; the boatman pulls it up.

Before the advent of pearl farms, more than
a ton of pearl oysters had to be collected by hand
to find 3 or 4 quality pearls.

4 The diver collects oysters and puts them in the basket.

5 When the diver needs to come up for air, she tugs on the rope, and the boatman pulls her up.

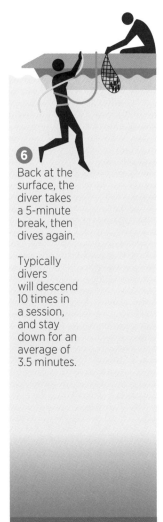

6 Back at the surface, the diver takes a 5-minute break, then dives again.

Typically divers will descend 10 times in a session, and stay down for an average of 3.5 minutes.

The seas around us

71% of the planet is covered with water, so perhaps we should all get to know a bit about it. The five named oceans are all connected, and that means we are in effect awash in a one big pond. Yet we know more about outer space than we do about the sea.

dry

wet

Five big questions that oceanographers are studying:

1 Why does the sea seem to be angry?

Global climate change is whipping up bigger and bigger storms. The 2004 Indian Ocean tsunami produced waves on land that reached 30m (100ft) high. 230,000 people died.

house

2 You're going to drink that?

With drinking water in short supply in many parts of the world, scientists are trying to find economic ways to desalinate the oceans. Today, the countries most active in getting the salt out of sea water are in the Middle East and North Africa, but it's expensive, and the cost has kept desalination from becoming widespread.

3 Anything living down here?

No human could withstand the pressure. Sorry, no mermaids. You couldn't see them anyway: there's no light after you've gone down more than 150m (500 ft). However, certain species of angler fish can survive; and with their bioluminescent* appendages they hunt for food in the Mariana Trench, in the Western Pacific, which is around 10km (6.2 miles) deep.

This is lifesize. Pretty small!

* Only one other animal with this facility: fireflies!

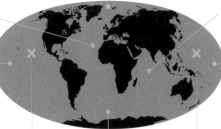

Arctic
14.1 million sq km (5.4 million sq miles)

Atlantic
76.8 million sq km
(29.7 million sq miles)

Indian
68.6 million sq km
(26.5 million sq miles)

Pacific
155.6 million sq km
(60 million sq miles)

Pacific (again!)

Southern (Antarctic)
20.3 million sq km
(7.8 million sq miles)

4 What's all that garbage? ✕

We throw a lot of stuff away. And **a lot of it** ends up in these two "garbage patches" in the Pacific.

Currents gather it into swirling masses of (mostly) plastic. It's only partly visible from the surface, but it's deadly to marine animals, which choke to death on our discarded shopping bags and non-biodegradable cups and water (!) bottles.

5 How deep is the ocean?

Average: 4.3km (2.6 miles)

The Challenger Deep, in the Mariana Trench, near Guam, is the **deepest: 11km (6.9 miles)**

If the highest mountain on land sat on the bottom of the ocean here, its summit would not reach the ocean's surface. (Mount Everest is 8.8km (5.5 miles) high.)

How to be a mountain guide

First thing: climbing is **dangerous** and takes time to master.
Begin with easy climbs and progress to harder climbs as you gain experience.

❶ Get fit!

It's very demanding. If you think you can just go climbing after sitting at a desk all day, I'm afraid you are wrong. Train for fitness and strength in ways that benefit you the best.

Try these fitness regimens:

 running and jogging, including endurance running

 walking and hiking, with the hiking getting increasingly arduous

 weightlifting, or walking/running with weights in a backpack or in your hands

 practising climbing on a local wall, or taking ice-climbing lessons

skiing or snow-boarding (especially if you intend to descend that way: extreme, but possible on some mountains!)

 anything that helps you **improve strength and endurance—** essentials for complete mountain-climbing fitness

❷ Be a safe climber: some tips

 Plan carefully: you must have information about the length and difficulty of your climb to be sure of a safe experience on the mountain. **Tell others where you are going.**

 Be realistic about your level of fitness, and choose suitable hikes or climbs. Start early in the morning and build extra time into your plan, to make sure you are back before it gets dark.

 Make sure you **take plenty of fluids:** water, tea or natural juices are the best. Take foods rich in nutrients, such as wholemeal bread, dried fruits and nuts.

 Before you go, study the **latest weather forecast.** Then keep watching conditions while you are climbing.

 Always follow the path and stay on marked trails. Consult your map: in case of doubt, turn back in good time.

Here we go!

③ Take the right gear

You'll need this **essential equipment** ➡️ to keep your clients (and yourself!) safe.

Belay device
Prevents climbers from falling

Grappling hook
This allows you to create a grip on the rock.

Carabiners
Different types and shapes have many uses (e.g., clip yourself or your gear to the rock face).

Helmet
Falling rock or chunks of ice can really spoil your day!

Backpack
Food and drink! Plus first aid kit. (Perhaps even a tent.)

Climbing rope
Attached to the rock wall as the lead climber goes up.

Harness
Worn snugly on the hips, it attaches climber to rope— it's a safety net. It's also used to carry gear.

Crampons
For extra grippage.

Walking the dog(s)

You might think that taking dogs for a walk would be fun, or be good exercise, or that it might turn into a job, but first you must really love dogs.

I mean, do you have a car sticker like this?

Starting out

1 **Ask friends** if you can walk their dogs so you can get a little practice. A little later, if it goes well, get references from the owners.

2 Some schools offer **dog-walking certification** (and some cities require it). Find out what's available in your area.

3 **Know your city** or local area. Check out what dog-walking laws apply to you. For instance, what to do about dog bites, and the importance of keeping rabies vaccinations up to date.

How many dogs can I take at one time?

4 If this is to be your business, think about how many dogs you can take on a walk at one time. **Start with just one or two.** When you have more confidence, perhaps you can go up to five.

5 You must learn **which breeds get on with others,** let alone the personalities (dogalties?) of the animals you group together.

The way to walk

6 Remember, **dogs are pack animals,** but you lead the pack! The dogs should walk beside or slightly behind you, but never in front. It's very important to show them that **you are the leader.**

7 **Do not let dogs off the leash,** except in special dog-run areas. And even then always keeps your dogs in your view.

8 In cold weather, wear warm clothes—but don't worry too much about the dogs, they naturally regulate their temperature.

9 Carry some **water** with you and a collapsible drinking bowl, especially on hot days. You never know what might keep you outside longer than you had planned. Of course, take plastic **poop bags** (more than one), and use them!

Woof, woofetty, woof.*

Translation:
"That looks like fun.
Can I join the pack?"

How to mend your bike

Apart from using lightweight carbon for the frame, bicycles haven't changed much since the 1880s—the double triangle *shape* of the frame has been only slightly modified since then.

Bicycles are pretty easy to fix, so often you can do the work yourself instead of taking the bike to a mechanic.

Such as:

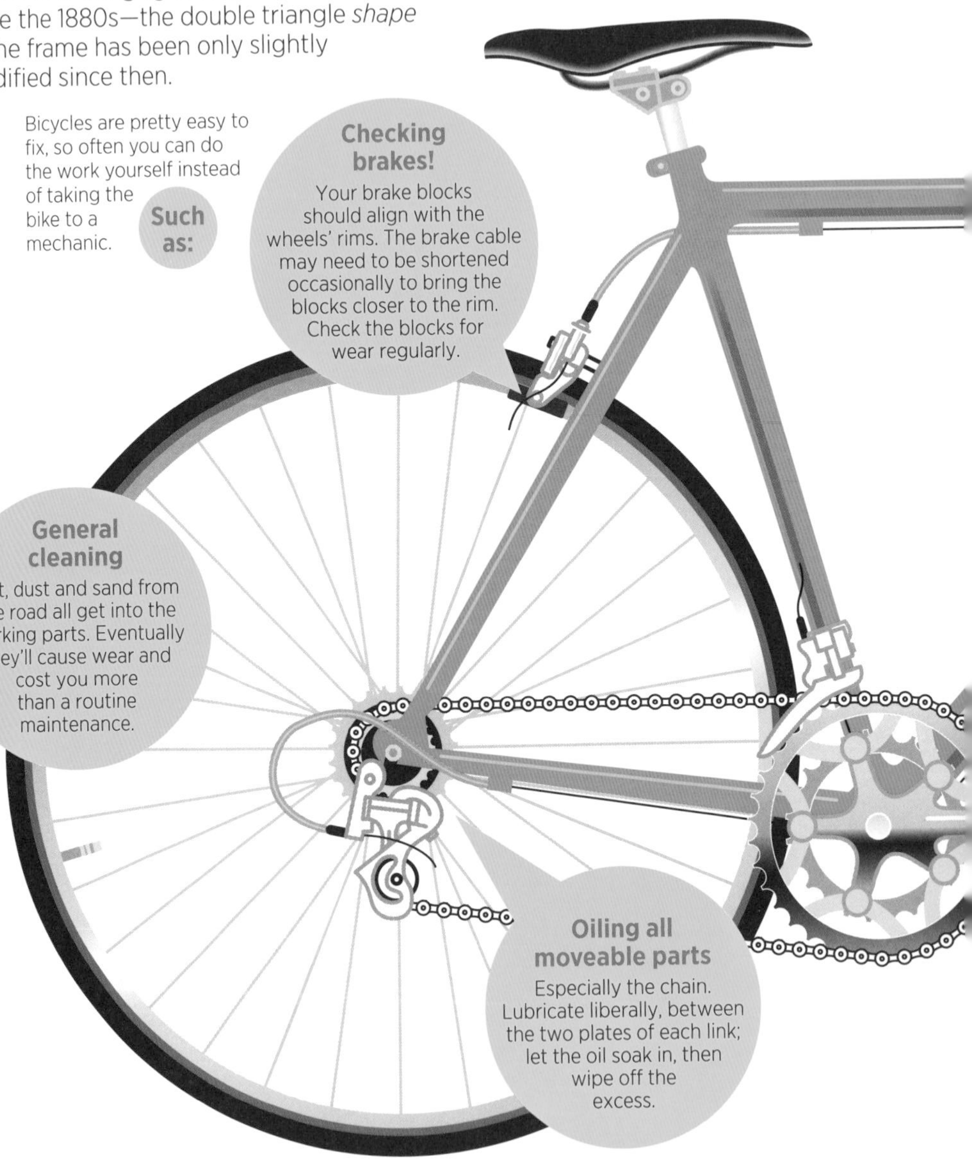

Checking brakes!

Your brake blocks should align with the wheels' rims. The brake cable may need to be shortened occasionally to bring the blocks closer to the rim. Check the blocks for wear regularly.

General cleaning

Grit, dust and sand from the road all get into the working parts. Eventually they'll cause wear and cost you more than a routine maintenance.

Oiling all moveable parts

Especially the chain. Lubricate liberally, between the two plates of each link; let the oil soak in, then wipe off the excess.

Watching
for worn-out
parts

**Checking
tyre pressure**
Too much pressure
causes as many flat
tyres as too little.
Check what's right
for this bike.

And...
Never overtighten
nuts. Get a torque
wrench to indicate
the correct
tension.

Next: **Fixing a flat** →

Fixing a flat

Not that difficult. You can do it!

1 Remove the wheel by undoing the quick release or the nuts holding it in the frame or fork. Don't try to save time by leaving it on the bike. You'll be sorry.

2 Insert a tyre lever under the tyre and hook it onto a spoke.

3 Insert a second tyre lever under the tyre.

4 Holding the first lever in place, drag the second one all the way round, so that one edge of the tyre is now outside the rim.

5 Pull the damaged innertube out.

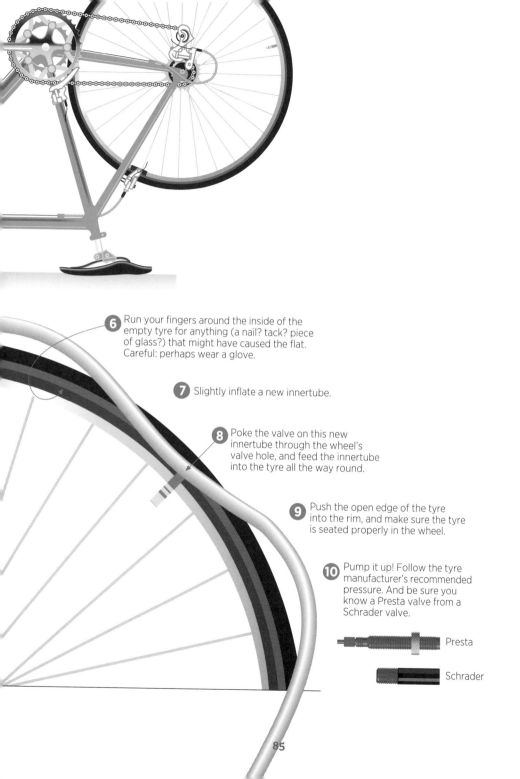

6 Run your fingers around the inside of the empty tyre for anything (a nail? tack? piece of glass?) that might have caused the flat. Careful: perhaps wear a glove.

7 Slightly inflate a new innertube.

8 Poke the valve on this new innertube through the wheel's valve hole, and feed the innertube into the tyre all the way round.

9 Push the open edge of the tyre into the rim, and make sure the tyre is seated properly in the wheel.

10 Pump it up! Follow the tyre manufacturer's recommended pressure. And be sure you know a Presta valve from a Schrader valve.

Presta

Schrader

Sailing the wrong way right

It seems anti-intuitive, but by sailing a boat into the wind, you can reach greater speeds than by sailing when the wind is pushing you. It's all about physics—first proposed by Daniel Bernoulli (1700–1782), a Swiss mathematician and physicist—the Bernoulli Principle.

Sailing into the wind

1 Wind "splits" as it hits the sails.

2 Wind flowing over the convex side of the billowed sail has a greater distance to cover than wind flowing across the other side of the sail.

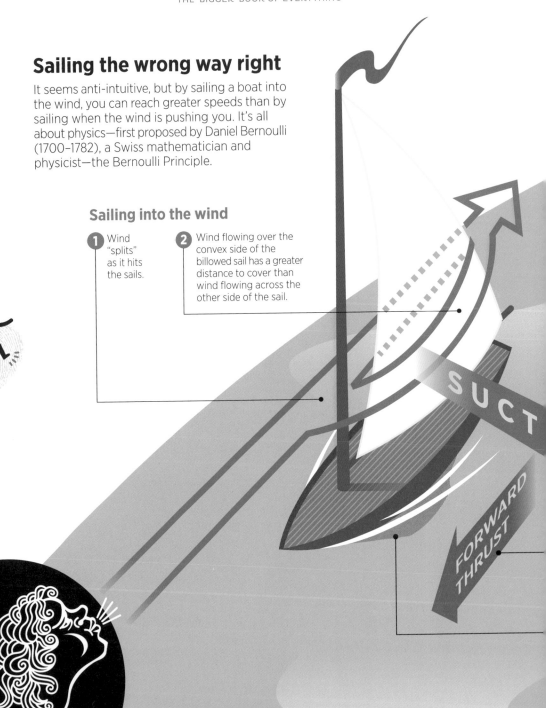

SUCT

FORWARD THRUST

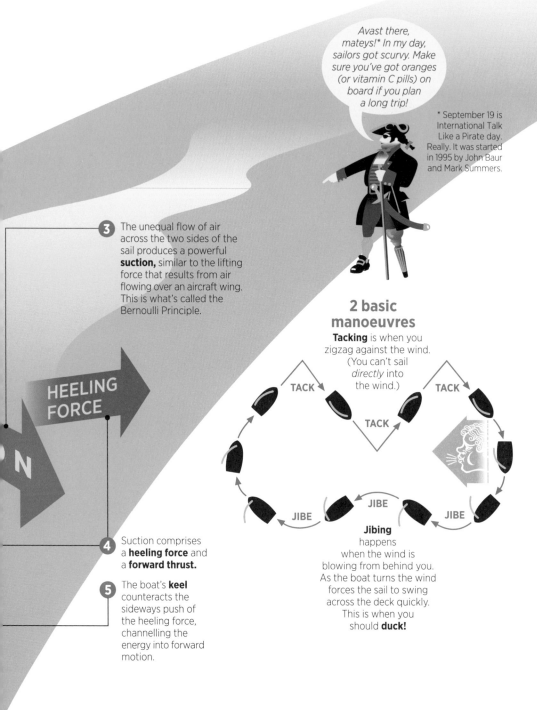

Avast there, mateys!* In my day, sailors got scurvy. Make sure you've got oranges (or vitamin C pills) on board if you plan a long trip!

* September 19 is International Talk Like a Pirate day. Really. It was started in 1995 by John Baur and Mark Summers.

3 The unequal flow of air across the two sides of the sail produces a powerful **suction,** similar to the lifting force that results from air flowing over an aircraft wing. This is what's called the Bernoulli Principle.

2 basic manoeuvres

Tacking is when you zigzag against the wind. (You can't sail *directly* into the wind.)

HEELING FORCE

N

TACK

TACK

TACK

JIBE

JIBE

JIBE

4 Suction comprises a **heeling force** and a **forward thrust.**

5 The boat's **keel** counteracts the sideways push of the heeling force, channelling the energy into forward motion.

Jibing happens when the wind is blowing from behind you. As the boat turns the wind forces the sail to swing across the deck quickly. This is when you should **duck!**

Oops!

You're bound to capsize sometime, so here's
how to right a small boat, and get back in.

Finally ...
how to drop anchor

 Lower sails
and roll
them up.

 **Find a spot
30m (100ft)
from other
boats,** and
away from cliffs
and sea walls, etc.

 Turn the boat to
face the wind or
current.

Yachtsman's
anchor

 Slowly **lower
the anchor**
over the bow
until it reaches
the bottom.

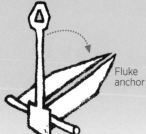

Fluke
anchor

5

If you have an **engine (or outboard motor), set it in reverse** and and move **slowly** away from the anchor until it bites.

6

Tie the rope (line) around the cleat with a **cleat hitch.**

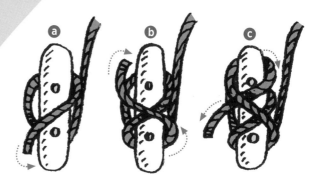

My friend says sailing is like taking a shower with your clothes on while you throw $100 bills down the drain.

Yeah, That's pretty much it.

Tying knots

Knowing knots is one of the first skills you need to make your boat secure, whether it's in dock or on the open water. Here are some of the basic knots, hitches and bends you should know. Practise with a bit of thick string.

QUICK GLOSSARY
Knot, hitch and bend are often used interchangeably, but their different definitions are useful.

A **knot,** when tied, remains a knot ...

... while a **hitch** is a knot tied around an object, and when the object is removed, the knot falls apart.

A **bend** is used to join the ends of two ropes together, like these two.

Sheet Bend
Used to join two ropes together.

Reef Knot
A simple way to tie the two ends of a rope together.
It also can be used as a bend to join two ropes.

WHEN A ROPE IS NOT A ROPE
In sailing, a **rope** is called a **line,** unless it is part of the sail's rigging, when it's called a **sheet**.
Got that?

Sailor's Knot
A secure way to attach a rope to an object.
But it's not a hitch because it remains a knot without the object.

Stevedore's Knot
When pulled tight, this makes a good stopper at the end of a rope.

Overhand Knot
The most basic of all knots. It's frequently used to make other knots and hitches.

Figure Eight Knot
(Also called: Flemish Knot; Savoy Knot)
The standard maritime knot, it can also be used as a decorative feature.

Clove Hitch
Used to tie a rope around an object.

Bowline
Use this to make a fixed loop at the end of a rope.
Two of these loops on one rope can be used to lift a person.

Lark's Head
Used to attach a rope to a ring or other object.

Timber Hitch
Used to attach a rope to a post or other object.

Lariat Loop
Commonly used on a lasso.
When there's a bull running wild on your boat, use this. Hey, you never know.

Slip Knot
(Also: Running Knot)
Attaches a rope to an object, closing around it when pulled tight.
The knot used by hangmen in America's Wild West.

Show me the way

If you want to be the navigator, you've got to know where you are going. But oops ... can't find your compass?

Fear not! Here are four ways to find what direction you are facing, without a compass.

during the day ...

1

Sunrise

- First thing in the morning, the sun is east-ish. But it varies through the year, sometimes actually rising in the east, but at others rising more towards the northeast or southeast.

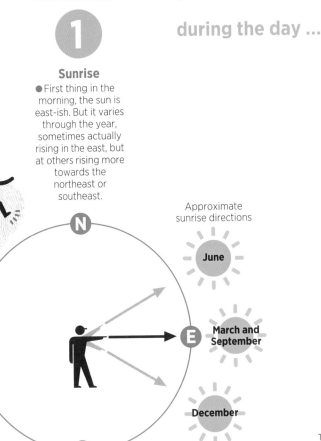

Approximate sunrise directions

June

March and September

December

2

Stick and shadow

- The shortest shadow cast by a stick is a perfect north-south line anywhere in the world, and this happens at midday.

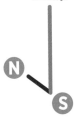

- It's the shortest shadow because the sun is highest in the sky at that time (whatever your watch might say!)—the sun is no longer east of you and has started setting to the west of you.

- Anywhere that's north of the Tropic of Cancer (that includes all of Europe and the US) the sun will be due south at midday.

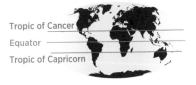

Tropic of Cancer

Equator

Tropic of Capricorn

- South of the Tropic of Capricorn it's the other way round.

3

or at night

4

Moon

- If the moon is in a crescent phase, imagine a line running from its top tip past the bottom tip and all the way down to earth's horizon.

- If you're in the Northern Hemisphere, the point where the line touches the ground is due south from where you are.

- In the Southern Hemisphere, where the line touches the ground is due north.

Stars

- Place a straight stick on a tall rock or tree limb. Make sure it's steady.

- Stand or lie in a position you can copy later.

Tip: mark the position of your fist on the rock so you always go back to exactly the same position.

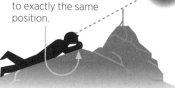

- Using the stick as a sight, line it up with a bright star that you can recognize later.

- Come back in half an hour and notice which direction the star has moved—

 if it's moved to the right, you are facing south.

 moved left, = facing north

 moved up, = facing east

 moved down, = facing west

The star may have moved up and right or down and right slightly, so you will have to estimate direction, such as southeast or southwest.

The Twin Otter turbine engine DC-3 is one of a small group of planes used for jumpers.

Jumping into the fire

Some brave people jump out of planes into a blazing fire zone. *On purpose.* They are specialist firefighters, called smokejumpers, whose job is to contain wildfires.

Smokejumpers have to be fit. In California* these are the **minimum physical requirements:**

- do 7 pull-ups
- do 25 push-ups
- do 45 sit-ups
- run 4.8km (1.5 miles) in 11 minutes
- carry 50kg (110lb) pack 3 miles in 90 minutes
  (They will be carrying their kit for days, perhaps weeks, in the wild.)

and they must:
- be at least 18 years old
- be a minimum of 1.5m (5ft) and a maximum of 2m (6ft 5in) tall
- weigh at least 55kg (120lbs) but no more than 90kg (200lbs)

*Smokejumpers operate mostly in the western US, and Russia.

Previous parachuting experience is neither required nor advantageous. But guts are needed.

There's a tough training period: smokejumpers are taught how to land in rough, forested terrain. (Part of the equipment they carry is a rope in case they land in a tree.)

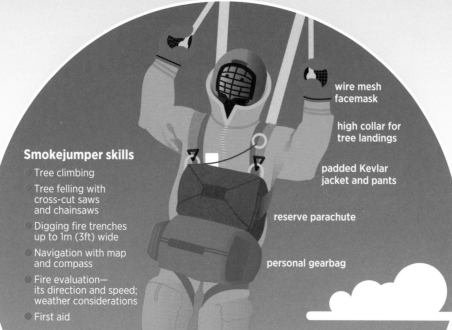

Smokejumper skills

- Tree climbing
- Tree felling with cross-cut saws and chainsaws
- Digging fire trenches up to 1m (3ft) wide
- Navigation with map and compass
- Fire evaluation— its direction and speed; weather considerations
- First aid

wire mesh facemask

high collar for tree landings

padded Kevlar jacket and pants

reserve parachute

personal gearbag

rope for tree landings in leg pockets

Mechanical saws, shovels, Pulaskis (half-pick, half axe) and McLeods (part rake, part shovel) are dropped into the firezone separately.

What climatologists do

Unlike TV weather forecasters, climatologists don't predict day-to-day weather. Their job is to research long-term processes.

Here are four signs of climate change that climatologists are urging us all to heed.

1 Perhaps the most important result of increasing temperatures is the rising ocean

- **Polar icecaps** have melted faster in the last 20 years than in the whole of the last 10,000. Scientists now say that this melt is unstoppable, and that sea levels could rise by 3 feet or more by 2100.

- **Coastal cities** in the US will be inundated. The **Maldive Islands** in the Indian Ocean will completely disappear.

- Many animal species are threatened, among them **Adélie penguins** on Antarctica, and **Polar bears** in the Arctic. They face extinction because their habitats are disappearing.

2 More rain (much more)

- Climatologists calculate that just in the US **global warming has put an extra 3.7 trillion litres (1 trillion gallons) of water into the air.**

- **This has to fall** as rain or snow, and that's why rain- and snow-storms will be more frequent and of greater ferocity.

3 Conflicts

- It's said that the next major war will be fought over **water rights, food and land.**

- Some experts believe that the conflict in **Darfur, Sudan,** was partially caused by a warmer climate—especially because it reduced natural resources, and that led to refugees fighting settled farmers for food sources.

4 Hunger

- Moderate warming and increased carbon (CO_2) in the atmosphere help plants grow faster, but if the warming trend continues at the current rate, **floods and drought will reduce crop yields.**

- **Fisheries** are adversely affected by warming water temperatures; this makes the water hospitable to invasive species and alters the timing of life cycles.

Much (not all) **of the warming trend is caused by the increasing quantities of CO_2 that we dump into the atmosphere.**

Here's how greenhouse gases heat Earth.

1 Sun's rays keep Earth at a liveable temperature.

2 Heat is reflected.

3 CO_2 builds up in the atmosphere, forming a **barrier** that sends some heat back to Earth again.

EARTH

ETIQUETTE

How to kiss!

It differs from country to country,
so make sure you know where you are.

Sometimes
you just rub
cheeks and
kiss the air.
(See USA.)

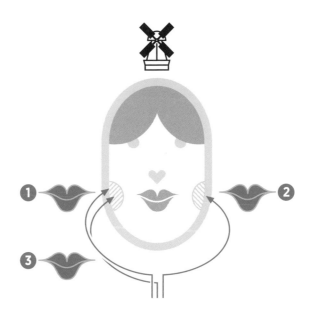

Here you really kiss the air.

Other worldly ways to say hello

Basic rule: **check with the locals** about what's done (and not done).

Here are a few pointers:

In the **United Arab Emirates,** men kiss other men three to four times on the cheeks.

In **Saudi Arabia,** men kiss on both cheeks after shaking hands.

In **Spain,** it's the same as in France, but you go to the right side first.

In **Africa,** some people kiss the ground when tribal leaders have just passed by.

Not much kissing in the **UK.** Just shake hands there.

Same thing in **Germany.**

Oh behave! (in England)

During your trip to London, you might get invited to Buckingham Palace. (OK, let's *pretend* you might get invited to Buckingham Palace.)

This is how to
curtsey to the Queen
when you meet her.
Please practise, because she does expect it.

The Queen doesn't actually wear a crown all the time, but lots of people would like it if she did.

102

At the end of a formal dinner, here's the **right way to pour and pass the port.**

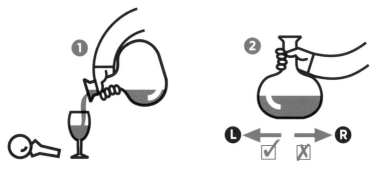

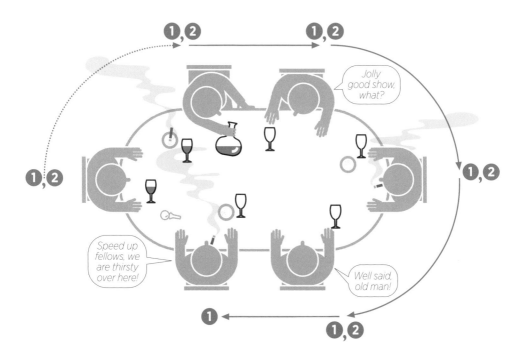

How to use chopsticks

Chopsticks originated in China in the Shang Dynasty (1600–1046 BCE) and were first used for cooking—the earliest ones found were bronze—not as eating utensils. In China, Taiwan, Japan, Korea and Vietnam there are variations in styles, materials and etiquette, but here's a basic guide to holding them, with some facts about history and manners.

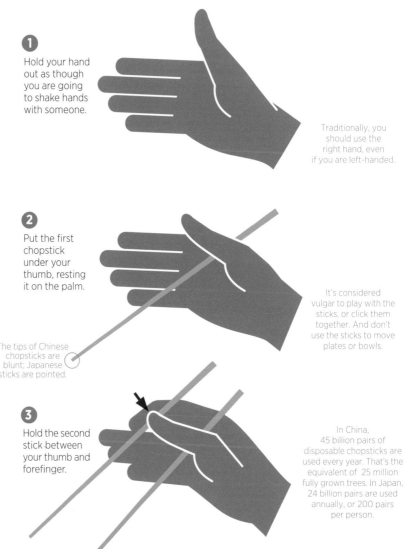

1

Hold your hand out as though you are going to shake hands with someone.

Traditionally, you should use the right hand, even if you are left-handed.

2

Put the first chopstick under your thumb, resting it on the palm.

It's considered vulgar to play with the sticks, or click them together. And don't use the sticks to move plates or bowls.

The tips of Chinese chopsticks are blunt; Japanese sticks are pointed.

3

Hold the second stick between your thumb and forefinger.

In China, 45 billion pairs of disposable chopsticks are used every year. That's the equivalent of 25 million fully grown trees. In Japan, 24 billion pairs are used annually, or 200 pairs per person.

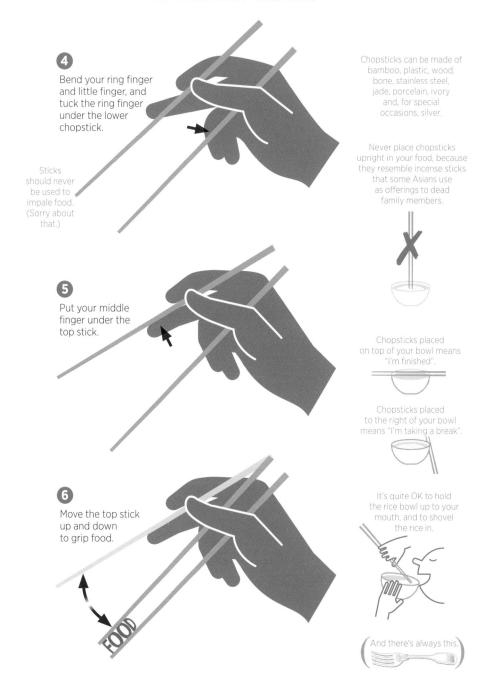

4 Bend your ring finger and little finger, and tuck the ring finger under the lower chopstick.

Sticks should never be used to impale food. (Sorry about that.)

Chopsticks can be made of bamboo, plastic, wood, bone, stainless steel, jade, porcelain, ivory and, for special occasions, silver.

Never place chopsticks upright in your food, because they resemble incense sticks that some Asians use as offerings to dead family members.

5 Put your middle finger under the top stick.

Chopsticks placed on top of your bowl means "I'm finished".

Chopsticks placed to the right of your bowl means "I'm taking a break".

6 Move the top stick up and down to grip food.

FOOD

It's quite OK to hold the rice bowl up to your mouth, and to shovel the rice in.

And there's always this.

How to wear a kilt

Everyone wants to know: **underpants or no underpants?** Sorry to squish a lovely story, but it's a myth that kilt wearers go without underneath. And since the formal kilt (the outfit shown here) is often worn where wild and informal dancing is likely to break out, wearing them is a good way to avoid embarrassment.

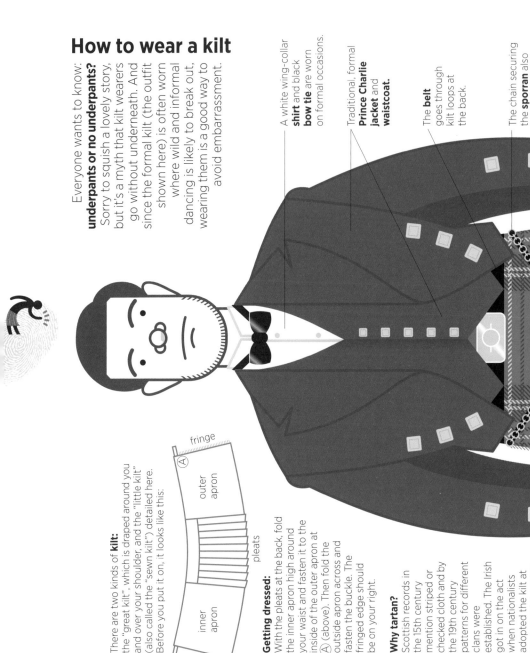

A white wing-collar **shirt** and black **bow tie** are worn on formal occasions.

Traditional, formal **Prince Charlie jacket** and **waistcoat.**

The **belt** goes through kilt loops at the back.

The chain securing the **sporran** also goes through the kilt loops.

fringe

ⓐ

outer apron

inner apron

pleats

There are two kinds of **kilt:** the "great kilt", which is draped around you and over your shoulder, and the "little kilt" (also called the "sewn kilt") detailed here. Before you put it on, it looks like this:

Getting dressed:
With the pleats at the back, fold the inner apron high around your waist and fasten it to the inside of the outer apron at ⓐ (above). Then fold the outside apron across and fasten the buckle. The fringed edge should be on your right.

Why tartan?
Scottish records in the 15th century mention striped or checked cloth and by the 19th century patterns for different clans were established. The Irish got in on the act when nationalists adopted the kilt at the turn of the 20th century.

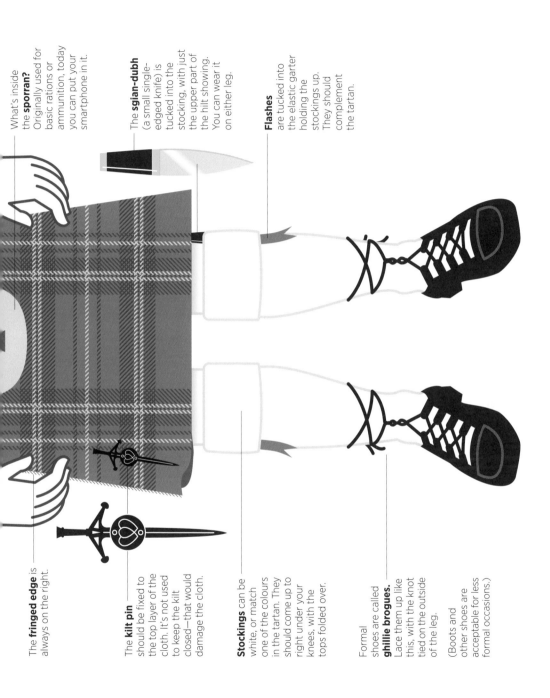

What's inside the **sporran?** Originally used for basic rations or ammunition, today you can put your smartphone in it.

The **sgian-dubh** (a small single-edged knife) is tucked into the stocking, with just the upper part of the hilt showing. You can wear it on either leg.

Flashes are tucked into the elastic garter holding the stockings up. They should complement the tartan.

The **fringed edge** is always on the right.

The **kilt pin** should be fixed to the top layer of the cloth. It's not used to keep the kilt closed—that would damage the cloth.

Stockings can be white, or match one of the colours in the tartan. They should come up to right under your knees, with the tops folded over.

Formal shoes are called **ghillie brogues.** Lace them up like this, with the knot tied on the outside of the leg.

(Boots and other shoes are acceptable for less formal occasions.)

Cultural no-nos

OOPS!

Other people's social customs can be very different from yours. Here are some pitfalls to watch out for.

 Your job?

OOPS!

It's rude to ask people in **Argentina** what they do for a living. Wait until they want to bring it up in conversation.

 Aaaatchoo!

OOPS!

In **Japan,** never blow your nose into a handkerchief. The Japanese word for snot is *hanakuso*, which translates to "nose shit", so they don't like the idea of anyone carrying it around with them.

 Giving flowers? Watch out!

OOPS!

Carnations are used at funerals in **Germany, Poland** and **Sweden.** Chrysanthemums are used at funerals in **Belgium, Italy, France, Spain** and **Turkey.**

 Giving flowers? Part two

OOPS!

It's unlucky to give odd numbers of flowers in **China** and **Indonesia,** but odd numbers of flowers are lucky in **Germany, India, Russia** and **Turkey.**

 Gloves off

OOPS!

In **Europe,** you'll be considered rude if you don't take your gloves off before shaking hands. (Even if it's freezing outside!)

 The bill

OOPS!

In restaurants in **Spain,** always request the bill at the end of a meal. Waiters think it's rude to bring it to you before you have asked for it.

Eye level

OOPS!

In **Scandinavia** and **Germany** you should look your fellow travellers in the eye when you are toasting. In **Russia,** drink the vodka in one gulp.

 Head matters

OOPS!

At holy places in **Thailand** and other Buddhist countries, never pat anyone on the head. The head is sacred.

Thumbing

The thumbs up sign is a rude gesture in **Egypt** and **Iran.**

 No thanks

As much as you might have enjoyed a meal in **India,** don't thank the host because saying "thank you" is seen as a form of payment, and may be taken as an insult.

 Foot blunder

In most of **Asia,** feet are thought of as being dirty, so it's disrespectful to point your feet or show the bottom of your shoes to anyone. Don't do it!

 Right is right

The left hand is considered the dirty hand in **Africa** and **India,** so use only your right hand when you eat.

 Palming

When getting a taxi in **Greece,** don't raise your hand as you would to signal *stop*. Greeks consider the forward-facing palm to be offensive, so turn your hand so that the palm is towards you (and keep the fingers together).

 Never leather

In **India,** don't give anyone a present made of leather, because cows are sacred. Also many people in India are vegetarian and may be offended by your gift.

 I didn't mean that!

In the **Philippines,** never refer to someone who has invited you to an event as your "hostess": it means "prostitute".

 Reading the cards

If you are on business in **Japan,** the business card exchange is a ritual you need to know about. Receive the card with both hands and a slight bow, then read it carefully. Never put it into your pocket or write on it.

 Wink, wink

Never wink at anyone in **India,** unless you know that it has sexual connotations!

How to visit a mosque

There are just a few rules, but it's very important that you respect them.

 Check ahead if non-Muslims may enter; some mosques may not always be open to non-Muslims. Friday is the day when it's most likely that you will not be allowed to visit. In certain cases, non-Muslims may have restricted access, or may not be allowed to enter at all.

(If you can't enter, you might be able to get a view of the mosque from elsewhere.)

Avoid entering during the calls to prayer (five times daily) unless you are a Muslim.

 Dress modestly—no shorts are allowed, and both men and women should cover their arms and backs.

Men should wear trousers, **not jeans.** Women must **cover their hair** with a headscarf, and wear a long skirt. Some mosques ask women to put on a cloak. (Headscarves and cloaks, if required, are usually provided.)

 Remove your shoes. Check at which point you should do this; as a general rule that will be when entering carpeted areas or the prayer hall.

 If you sit on the carpet, **make sure your feet are tucked behind you**—it is offensive to Muslims to have the soles of your feet pointed at them.

Photos: check if you are allowed to use your camera and if you can, be discreet.

Don't smoke.

Take care not to touch the Quran.

What is the "muezzin's call"?

- The muezzin is the chosen person at the mosque to summon Muslims to prayer at Friday services and the five daily times for prayer—at dawn, noon, midafternoon, sunset and nightfall (about two hours after sunset).

- The muezzin faces the direction of Mecca as he delivers the call from the minaret.

- The office of muezzin in cities is sometimes given to a blind man who cannot see down into the inner courtyards of citizens' houses, thus avoiding any possibility of intrusion into people's privacy.

- In most modern mosques the call *(adhan)* is electronically amplified.

- Egypt has introduced a controversial centralised muezzin: a single voice is broadcast live to the 4000 mosques in Cairo.

The call

❝ *Allah is most great. I testify that there is no God but Allah. I testify that Muhammad is the prophet of Allah. Come to prayer. Come to salvation. Allah is most great. There is no God but Allah.* **❞**

The melodious chanting of the *adhan* is considered an art form.

Want some fun?

When it comes to a holiday romance, you'll do a lot better if you ask nicely and in the right language. Here's **how to chat people up (and turn them down)!**

In French:

Do you want to go out with me?
Veux-tu sortir avec moi?
ver•tew sor•teer a•vek mwa

I love you.
Je t'aime.
zher•tem

Would you like to do something?
Est-ce que tu aimerais faire quelque chose?
es•ker tew em•ray fair kel•ker shoz

Yes, I'd love to.
Oui, j'aimerais bien.
wee zhem•ray byun

Would you like a drink?
Si on buvait quelque chose?
see on bew•vay kel•ker shoz

Shall we get some fresh air?
Nous allons prendre l'air?
noo za•lon pron•drer lair

Leave me alone, please.
Laissez-moi tranquille, s'il vous plaît.
lay•say•mwa trong•keel seel voo play

I'm sorry, I can't.
Non, je suis désolé(e), je ne peux pas.
non zher swee day•zo•lay zher ner per pa

Not if you were the last person on earth!
Jamais de la vie!
zha•may der la vee

I like you very much.
Je t'aime beaucoup.
zher tem bo•koo

You're very attractive.
Tu es trés beau/belle.
tew ay tray bo/bel

I'm interested in you.
Je m'intéresse vraiment á toi.
zher mun•tay•res vray•mon a twa

You're great.
Tu es formidable.
tew ay for•mee•da•bler

Let's go to bed!
On va se coucher!
on va ser koo•shay

Kiss me.
Embrasse-moi.
om•bras•mwa

Excuse me, I have to go now.
Excusez-moi, je dois partir maintenant.
ek•skyew•zay•mwa zher dwa par•teer mun•ter•non

No, thank you.
Non, merci.
non mair•see

I'd rather not.
Je n'ai pas trés envie.
zher nay pa tray zon•vee

In Russian:

Would you like to do something?
kha•tit•ye peyd•yom ku•da•ni•butí

I love you.
ya lyub•lyu tib•ya

Would you like a drink?
kha•tit•ye vih•pití sa mnoy

What are you having?
shto vih kha•tit•ye pití

You look great!
vih klas•na vih•gli•dit•ye

I want to get to know you better.
mnye bih khat•ye•lasí uz•natí a tib•ye pa•bolí•she

Can I kiss you?
mozh•na tib•ya pat•se•la•vatí

Do you want to come inside for a while?
kho•chishí zey•ti na vryem•ya

Can I stay over?
mozh•na mnye a•stati•sa

Kiss me.
pat•se•luy min•ya

Let's go to bed.
da•vey f past•yelí

Excuse me, I have to go now.
iz•vi•nit•ye mnye pa•ra i•ti

Leave me alone!
pri•va•li•vey

Sorry, I can't.
sa•zhal•ye•ni•yu ya nye ma•gu

Piss off!
at•ye•bisí

In Italian:

I love you.
Ti amo.
tee a•mo

Would you like a drink?
Prendi qualcosa da bere?
pren•dee kwal•ko•za da be•re

Can I dance with you?
Posso ballare con te?
po•so ba•la•re kon te

Shall we get some fresh air?
Andiamo a prendere
un po'd'aria fresca?
an•dya•mo a pren•de•re
oon po da•rya fres•ka

Can I sit here?
Posso sedermi qui?
po•so se•der•mee kwee

Can I kiss you?
Ti posso baciare?
tee po•so ba•cha•re

Will you take me home?
Mi porti a casa?
mee por•tee a ka•za

Let's go to bed!
Andiamo a letto!
an•dya•mo a le•to

**I'm sorry, but I
don't feel like it.**
Mi dispiace ma
non ne ho voglia.
mee dees•pya•che ma
non ne o vo•lya

I'm not interested.
Non mi interessa.
non mee een•te•re•sa

Leave me alone!
Lasciami in pace!
la•sha• mee een pa•che

In German:

Haven't we met before?
Kennen wir uns nicht von
irgendwoher?
ke•nen veer uns nikht fon
ir•gent•vo•hair

Would you like a drink?
Möchtest du etwas trinken?
merkh•test doo et•vas
tring•ken

**You have a beautiful
personality.**
Du hast eine wundervolle
Persönlichkeit.
doo hast ai•ne vun•der•
vo•ler per•zern•likh•kait

Kiss me.
Küss mich.
kus mikh

Let's go to bed!
Gehen wir ins Bett!
gay•en veer ins bet

**Excuse me, I have
to go now.**
Tut mir Leid, ich muss
jetzt gehen.
toot meer lait ikh mus
yetst gay•en

No, thank you.
Nein, danke.
nain dang•ke

I'd rather not.
Lieber nicht.
lee•ber nikht

Perhaps some other time.
Vielleicht ein andermal.
fi•laikht ain an•der•mahl

Leave me alone!
Lass mich zufrieden!
las mikh tsu•free•den

In Spanish:

Would you like to do something?
¿Quieres hacer algo?
kye•res a•ther al•go

I love you.
Te quiero.
te kye•ro

Would you like a drink?
¿Te apetece una copa?
te a•pe•te•the oo•na ko•pa

You're great.
Eres estupendo/a.
e•res es•too•pen•do/a

Can I kiss you?
¿Te puedo besar?
te pwe•do b••sar

**Do you want to come
inside for a drink?**
¿Quieres entrar a tomar algo?
kye•res en•trar a to•mar al•go

Let's go to bed!
¡Vamonos a la cama!
va•mo•nos a la ka•ma

Excuse me, I have to go now.
Lo siento, pero me tengo que ir.
lo syen•to pe•ro me ten•go
ke eer

Leave me alone, please.
Déjame en paz, por favor.
de•kha•me en path por fa•vor

Go away!
¡Vete!
ve•te

**Hey, I'm not interested in
talking to you.**
Mira tĺo/a, es que no me
interesa hablar contigo.
mee•ra tee•o/a es ke no me
een•te•re•sa ab•lar kon•tee•go

Tipping tips

These are just guidelines, because tipping experts have differing opinions about some of the details. **Best advice: ask a local.** Unless you are on a really tight budget, why not give the waiter something when he or she is nice to you, even if this list suggests you don't have to. It's friendly to say thank you.

 Restaurants   Taxis  Typically not required   Typically included   Loose change   Highest Lowest

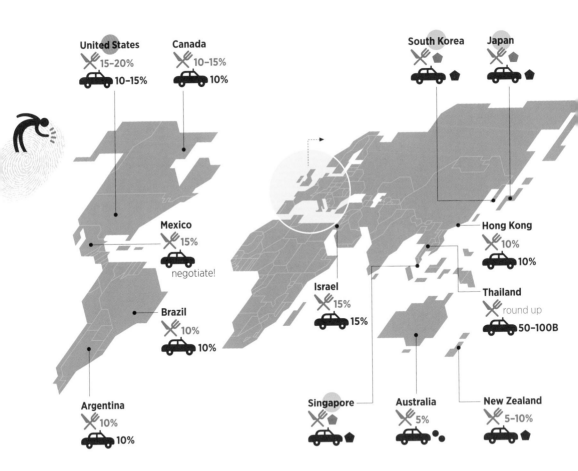

United States
15–20%
10–15%

Canada
10–15%
10%

South Korea

Japan

Mexico
15%
negotiate!

Hong Kong
10%
10%

Israel
15%
15%

Thailand
round up
50–100B

Brazil
10%
10%

Argentina
10%
10%

Singapore

Australia
5%

New Zealand
5–10%

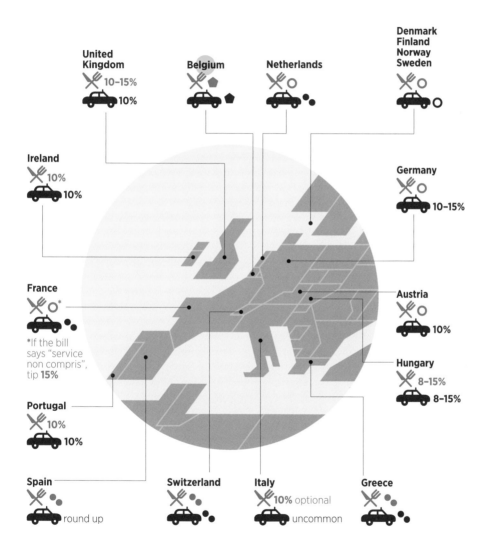

United Kingdom 10–15% 10%

Belgium

Netherlands

Denmark Finland Norway Sweden

Ireland 10% 10%

Germany 10–15%

France *
*If the bill says "service non compris", tip **15%**

Austria 10%

Hungary 8–15% 8–15%

Portugal 10% 10%

Spain round up

Switzerland

Italy **10%** optional uncommon

Greece

FOOD & DRINK

How to open a beer with a spoon

Don't worry if you can't find the bottle opener. Using a variety of everyday metal objects* (such as a spoon), the cap can easily be removed.

You can also do it with your teeth, but it's not recommended.

1 Grip the neck of the bottle firmly at the top, and put your thumb on the cap.

2 Resting the bowl of the spoon on your forefinger, hook the spoon under the cap.

* If there's no spoon around, you can also try these as levers to get the top off:

belt buckle
fork
car seatbelt latch
metal nail clippers
hammer
back of chef's knife

the horse's mouth

pale ale

the horse's mouth

pale ale

3 With your finger as a fulcrum, push down hard on the handle of the spoon to flip the cap off.

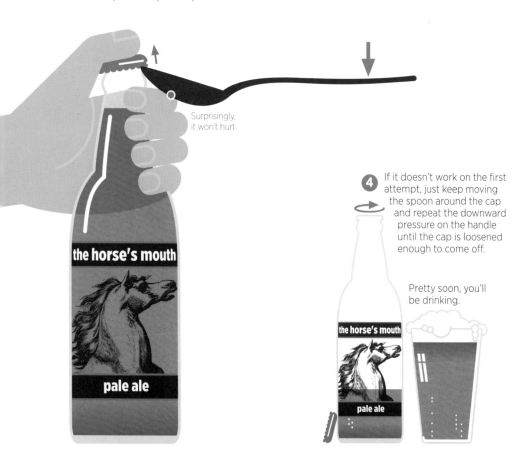

Surprisingly, it won't hurt.

4 If it doesn't work on the first attempt, just keep moving the spoon around the cap and repeat the downward pressure on the handle until the cap is loosened enough to come off.

Pretty soon, you'll be drinking.

the horse's mouth

pale ale

How to open a coconut
Smash it or tap it?

Brute force

1 There are **three dark indentations** at the blunt end of a coconut: two "eyes" and a "mouth", forming a triangle. They are the weakest parts of the outer shell.

3 Drive a strong, sharp object, such as a nail or screwdriver, into **two** of the holes (one is to let air in). Wiggle the objects a bit and remove.

2 **Nestle** the coconut into a folded TowEL.

4 Turn the coconut over and place on a glass to **drain** the coconut water.

The clear liquid is a popular drink in the tropics. Recent marketing claims for its health benefits are mostly unfounded.

5 Put the coconut in a plastic bag, and **whack** it.

TOWEL

6 You can keep the bits in the fridge for up to 7 days, or in the freezer for 3 months.

A gentler approach

1 With the coconut in your hand, use the back of a kitchen knife to **tap** the edge of the coconut around **its "equator".**

2 **Rotate** as you tap. Eventually it will split into two pieces. You might lose some of the water.

(If you don't have a knife handy, try tapping the coconut on the edge of a brick or rock.)

Optional (if you are at home, not on the beach)

3 Here's a way to loosen the flesh inside. Before doing the tapping, **bake** the coconut (at 93°C/200°F) for 15 minutes. Or put it in the **freezer** for 15 minutes.

If you do this, the inner husk will easily come away from the outer husk once it's opened.

4 The best way to remove the inner husk is to use a **potato peeler.**

And if you are in the jungle

5 Since you might not have any tools available, this could be a good way to open it.

Impale the blunt end of the coconut onto a strong, sharp stick.

Nice and shady but potentially dangerous.

How do you say Cheers! in China?

A phonetic pronunciation guide
to toasting around the world.

Albania — geh-zoo-ah

Armenia (West) — genatzt

Bosnia and Herzegovina — zhee-vi-lee

Brazil — sah-uh-ji

Bulgaria — naz-dra-vey

Myanmar (Burma) — au-ng my-in par say

China (Mandarin) — gan bay

Croatia — zhee-ve-lee / naz-dra-vlee

Czech Republic — naz-drah vi

Denmark — skoal

Egypt — fe sahetek

England — cheers

Estonia — ter-vih-sex

Finland — kippis

France — ah vot-re sahn-tay

Germany — prost

Greece — yamas

Guam (Chamorro) — bih-bah

Hawaii — okole maluna

Hungary — eggesh ay-ged-reh

Iceland — sk-owl

Ireland (Gaelic) — sławn-cha

Israel — l'chaim

It's thought that touching glasses
started as a way to make sure the drinks
were not poisoned. (One drink might spill over
into the other.) Another story suggests that the word
toast is connected to a 17th-century French custom of
flavouring drinks with spiced toast. Or perhaps a long
forgotten Henry Toast named the custom after himself.

Italy *sa-lutay*

Japan *kan-pie*

Korea *gun bae*

Latvia *pree-eh-ka*

Lithuania *ee-sewh-kata*

Macedonia *na zdravye*

Mongolia *er-uhl mehdiin toloo*

Netherlands *prohst*

Norway *skawl*

Philippines *mah-boo-hay*

Poland *naz-droh-vee-ay*

Portugal *s-ow-oo-der*

Romania *no-rock*

Russia *naz-dorovie*

Spain *sah-lud*

Sweden *skawl*

South Africa (Afrikaans) *ge-sund-hate*

Thailand *choc tee*

Turkey *sher-i-feh*

Ukraine *boodmo*

Vietnam *jou*

Wales *yeh-chid-dah*

*Here's to a long life,
and may you live a thousand years,
and I a thousand years less one day.
For I would not care to live,
after you had passed away.*

Drink up!

Here are a few ideas about how the word "cocktail" came about:

● It was the custom to put a feather (from a cock's tail) into the drink to alert non-drinkers that it contained alcohol.

● It's derived from the French word *"coquetier"*. A coquetier was an eggcup used in New Orleans in the 19th century to serve certain drinks.

● It's derived from the Latin *aqua decocta* meaning distilled water.

● Since cocktails were once a morning drink, it's a metaphor for the rooster waking us up.

● Colonial taverns in the USA used to keep spirits of all kinds in wooden casks, and as the level of the liquid went down, the spirits lost some of their flavour and potency. The inn-keeper poured the "tailings" from different casks into one from which he could sell drinks at a reduced price to boozers who asked for "cock tailings".

I don't care. You?

Not now I have a martini.

Doing shots

To keep things simple, all the ingredients in the drinks shown here are measured in shots. (Sounds a bit odd for juices, etc, but it's easier to keep the measures all the same.)

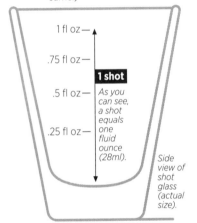

1 fl oz —

.75 fl oz —

1 shot

.5 fl oz —

As you can see, a shot equals one fluid ounce (28ml).

.25 fl oz —

Side view of shot glass (actual size).

What does "proof" mean?

Proof is the measurement of alcoholic strength. One degree of proof equals half a percent of alcohol, so if you've got a bottle that's 75 proof, it is 35% alcohol; if the bottle says 100 proof, it has 50% alcohol in it. (There are many kinds of alcohol, but only ethyl alcohol is in wine, beer and spirits.)

Wine ranges from 12% to 20% alcohol; lager beer is around 4% to 5%; a few beers go up to 9%. The wonderful Thomas Hardy's Ale is 11.7%, and I guess that's why it comes in small bottles. Cough suppressants can be as high as 25%.

Each of these makes one drink.

MARTINI

1.5 shots vodka or gin
dash dry vermouth
Shaken in ice;
add olives on a stick.
(Cocktail onions in gin make this a **Gibson.**)

COSMOPOLITAN

2 shots vodka
1 shot Cointreau
1 shot cranberry juice
juice of half a lime
Shaken in ice.

PINA COLADA

1 shot light rum
3 shots pineapple juice
1 shot coconut cream
soda water
Put in blender with
crushed ice; blend;
add cherries and
pineapple cubes on a stick.

CAIPIRINHA

1.5 shots cachaça
1 teaspoon sugar
half lime cut into wedges
4–5 mint leaves
Muddle lime, sugar and
mint until lime is juiced
and sugar liquefied; add
cachaça; shake well in
cocktail shaker; pour
into a rocks glass with ice.

MOJITO

1.5 shots light rum
2 shots soda water
1 teaspoon sugar
half lime cut into wedges
4–5 mint leaves
Muddle lime, sugar and
mint in a tall glass filled
with crushed ice;
add rum; top with
soda water; stir well.

WHISKY SOUR

1.5 shots whisky / juice of a lemon / 0.5 teaspoons sugar / Shake with ice; add a cherry, or olives, or a slice of lemon, lime or orange, or even a dash Angostura bitters.

The ingredients and quantities here are not set in stone. The amount of liquor in all cocktails can be varied to suit your taste: stronger, weaker or spicier.

MINT JULEP

2 shots bourbon
bunch of fresh mint
1 shot simple syrup*
Muddle 4–5 mint leaves with simple syrup in a glass; fill glass with crushed ice. Add bourbon, stir well; add more ice and stir again until ice forms on the outside of the glass. Push mint sprigs into the crushed ice so the top of the glass is entirely covered in mint.

*Simple syrup
Equal parts water and sugar.
Heat the water until it simmers; add the sugar. Don't let the mixture boil, but stir until the sugar is completely dissolved. Remove from heat and allow to cool.

SINGAPORE SLING

1.5 shots gin
0.5 shot cherry liqueur
0.25 shot Cointreau
0.25 shot Bénédictine
0.25 shot Grenadine
4 shots pineapple juice
1 shot lemon juice
dash Angostura bitters
Shaken in ice.

SIDECAR

1 shot Rémy Martin
0.5 shot Cointreau
1 lemon
sugar
Rim glass with lemon juice and sugar; put the glass in the freezer. Squeeze and strain lemon into a shaker; add liquor and ice; shake well; pour into frozen glass.

It's called a sidecar because you pour the balance of the mixture into a small glass placed beside the cocktail glass (for a refill).

BLUE HAWAIIAN

1 shot light rum
2 shots pineapple juice
1 shot blue Curaçao
1 shot coconut cream
Blend with ice in tall glass; decorate with a pineapple slice and a cherry.

SCREWDRIVER

1.5 shots vodka
4.5 shots orange juice
With ice in tall glass.

BLOODY MARY

1.5 shots vodka
3 shots tomato juice
0.5 shot lemon juice
dash Worcestershire sauce
dash hot sauce
1 teaspoon horseradish
pinch salt & pepper
With ice in tall glass; add a celery stick.

Wine scents

Trying to describe the taste of wine is hard. In 1984, Professor Ann Noble of the University of California developed an **aroma wheel** and there are now many different wheels in use.* Here's a simplified linear version. Soon you'll be able to **join the wine snobs and talk like a pro!**

Most of what we think we are tasting in wine (and food) is actually what we can **smell.** In fact, our tongues have receptors for just **five** basic tastes, while our noses can distinguish between 4,000 and 10,000 aromas.

- BITTER
- UMAMI (eg meat, MSG)
- SOUR
- SALT
- SWEET

In wine circles, **aroma** is the term applied to the smell that new wines acquire from their grapes.

Bouquet is technically the smell of the wine after it has developed and aged in the bottle. However, many people continue to use the term "aroma" after the bottle is opened (that's why the aroma wheel is called that).

*Google **aroma wheel** to see lots of examples of aroma charts and wheels.

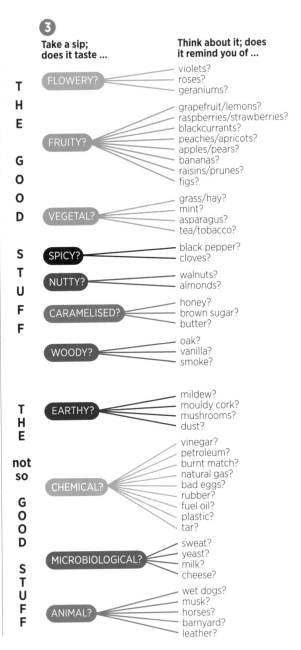

Take a sip; does it taste ...

Think about it; does it remind you of ...

THE GOOD STUFF

FLOWERY?
- violets?
- roses?
- geraniums?

FRUITY?
- grapefruit/lemons?
- raspberries/strawberries?
- blackcurrants?
- peaches/apricots?
- apples/pears?
- bananas?
- raisins/prunes?
- figs?

VEGETAL?
- grass/hay?
- mint?
- asparagus?
- tea/tobacco?

SPICY?
- black pepper?
- cloves?

NUTTY?
- walnuts?
- almonds?

CARAMELISED?
- honey?
- brown sugar?
- butter?

WOODY?
- oak?
- vanilla?
- smoke?

THE not so GOOD STUFF

EARTHY?
- mildew?
- mouldy cork?
- mushrooms?
- dust?

CHEMICAL?
- vinegar?
- petroleum?
- burnt match?
- natural gas?
- bad eggs?
- rubber?
- fuel oil?
- plastic?
- tar?

MICROBIOLOGICAL?
- sweat?
- yeast?
- milk?
- cheese?

ANIMAL?
- wet dogs?
- musk?
- horses?
- barnyard?
- leather?

Here are some amusing tests you can try with your drinking buddies.

Is it **WHITE** or is it RED ?

First blindfold a couple of people. Then give them a glass of red wine and ask if they can tell you if it's red or white. Then do the opposite and give them a glass of white and see if they know. (You'll be surprised at the answers.)

Next, out of sight of your friends, put two drops of red food colouring and one drop of blue food colouring into a full-bodied white wine (such as a chardonnay). Take off the blindfolds and give the drinkers a glass of this mixture and then a glass of red wine and see if they can tell the difference.

Many professional wine experts have failed both these tests.

Seasoned drinkers will soon catch on that the smell is the easiest way to tell the difference, but when we can *see* the colour it's amazing how much we are conditioned by what the wine looks like. Try it!

You know, we were making wine in Egypt about 5,000 years ago.

Really? Did *you* know that treading grapes is illegal in some parts of the US nowadays?

How to prevent a hangover ...

Everyone has a pet way to do this.
Here's a collection of remedies. Take your pick.

BEFORE DRINKING

1 **Eat fried food;** it makes you absorb alcohol more slowly (though you will eventually absorb it all).

2 **Drink milk;** it lines the stomach.

WHILE DRINKING

1 **Drink water** between alcoholic drinks.

2 **Eat something** while you drink. OK, not exactly *while* you drink, that could be messy. (Or fun, depending on how the evening is going.)

The bad and the better
The old saying "beer before wine, you'll be fine" is cute, but the order in which you drink different things really doesn't make any difference. It's the *amount* you consume that makes you drunk.

This is the order of hangover-makingness:

BAD
Your hangover will probably be worse if you drink spirits that have a deep colour.

 brandy

red wine

rum

whisky

white wine

gin

vodka

beer

BETTER

 water (designated driver)

or cure one

AT BEDTIME

1 Drink a lot of **water.**

2 Take **two Alka-Seltzer.**

3 **Close curtains,** or pull down blinds so room is dark in the morning.

Portrait of El Lissitzky with a hangover.

IN THE MORNING

(An old Irish custom: to cure a hangover, bury the ailing person up to the neck in moist sand.)

What you are feeling is the effects of dehydration, caused by alcohol.

DO this:

1 **Sleep longer,** if you have the time. (That's why you shut the light out.)

2 **Add a lemon slice** (for vitamin C) **to room-temperature water** and drink.

3 Drink **juice** for more vitamin C. (Tomato juice is good too.)

4 Eat plain, **burnt toast** (the carbon acts as a kind of filter); it boosts your blood sugar.

5 Eat **fruit** (bananas are good), a bacon sandwich, any mineral-rich food, such as pickles or canned fish.

6 **Take aspirin or ibuprofen** (note "don'ts" below).

7 **Shower.** Sounds obvious, but works wonders.

8 Go for a **walk.**

DON'T try any of these:

1 **Hair of the dog.** Many swear by the idea that a little more of what you had the night before will solve your problem. It might disguise your aching head a little, but it won't help cure it!

2 **Paracetamol-based pills** (these put even more strain on your liver and kidney).

3 **Hangover pills;** few work. And diet sodas or soft drinks don't help.

4 **Coffee:** it'll dehydrate you more.

5 **Any dairy products:** they'll make you feel more queasy.

☕ We love coffee ...

The world consumes **2.3 billion cups a day,** and there are many ways to drink it. For instance, here are six of the many **espresso** variations:

carajillo	cortado	doppio	guillermo	macchiato	affogato (more of a dessert!)
espresso + brandy	espresso + milk	double espresso	espresso + lime	espresso + foamed milk	espresso + ice cream

☕ How much?

These average prices for a **regular cup of coffee** are from a recent survey. Prices vary, of course, according to world market fluctuations and crop shortages, among other factors.

MOSCOW	$10.20
PARIS	$6.80
ATHENS	$6.60
BEIJING	$6.28
BERLIN	$5.20
TOKYO	$5.05
NEW YORK CITY	$3.80
JOHANNESBURG	$2.40
BUENOS AIRES	$2.00
SEOUL	50¢

All prices are US$.

☕ A very short history

The **Chinese discovered the effects of caffeine,** in the form of medicinal tea, about **5,000 years ago.** Coffee was introduced to Europe at the beginning of the 1600s. By the early 1700s, **Bach** had written his *Coffee Cantata* operetta while intellectuals such as Voltaire and Rousseau, frequenters of Paris's many coffee houses, praised the drink's ability to keep them "Enlightened".

and *why* we love it: caffeine!

☕ What is caffeine?

It's a stimulant found in more than 60 plants, including coffee beans and tea leaves. In its pure form, it's a white, bitter-tasting crystalline powder. The chemical structure, first identified in 1819, is nearly identical to that of **adenosine,** a chemical in the brain that slows activity and helps to regulate sleep.

☕ How does it work?

Since the molecular structure of caffeine is very similar to that of adenosine, **caffeine "poses" as adenosine** in the flow of messages from one brain cell to the next.

1 When there's no caffeine present, adenosine (◉) can flow unrestricted from one brain cell to receptors on the adjoining cell.

end of one
brain cell

receptor
sites on next
brain cell

2 But when caffeine (◉) is present, it fits perfectly into the receptors, fooling the brain cell and effectively suppressing the calming action of the adenosine.

3 With the adenosine blocked, more neurons start firing in the brain. This increased activity triggers the production of adrenaline, which causes your pupils to dilate, your heart to beat faster, and your blood pressure to rise. Your liver releases fatty acids and sugar into the bloodstream, giving you extra energy.

☕ How long does it stay in your system?

If you have a cup of coffee with 200mg of caffeine in it at 9am, there will still be 100mg of caffeine left in your body at 3pm.

200
mg

100
mg

How to roll a burrito

And what to put inside it before you do!

1

Put a **corn tortilla** on a plate and spread some **sour cream** in the middle of it.

2

Put some small pieces of cooked **chicken** (alternatively, **black beans** or **tofu**) onto the sour cream, and a dollop of **salsa*** *(see recipe on next page)* on top of that.

Fold the bottom edge of the tortilla towards the centre.

You can add **hot sauce** at any stage while you are making the burrito. But **beware,** there are some real mouth blasters out there. Try a drop before you go wild with the bottle.

Making the filling

It's easier if you use already-cooked chicken chopped into small chunks.

Put the chunks of chicken **(or a vegetarian alternative)** into a saucepan, and add: **cumin, hot chilli powder, a little salt, paprika and minced garlic.**

Toss with the spicy mix to coat the pieces. Then add a little water to the pan and gently heat through.

Fold one side of the
tortilla into the centre.

Roll the whole thing
into a tube that's open
at one end.

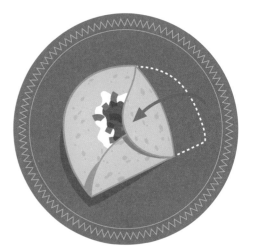

*For the salsa
Mix:
**chopped tomatoes,
coriander (cilantro) or
parsley, hot peppers
and onions, minced garlic
and oil.**

It doesn't matter if
you make
too much—it will
keep in the fridge for
a week or so.
(And it always seems
to get better
with age.)

 Try adding some
guacamole at step ❷ .

For that, mash together:
**chopped tomatoes, coriander (cilantro), onions
and ripe avocados, with a little lemon
or lime juice.**

If you chop the ingredients
really finely before mashing, you'll get
a smooth green guacamole. But if you
chop everything coarsely, and go light on
the mashing, you'll end up with a chunky mix.
Both are nice.

(This will keep for a couple of days in the
fridge. It will turn a rather unattractive
brown, but it's OK to eat.)

Want a thrill? Eat fugu. Carefully!

The fish

● The **fugu** (from two Chinese characters meaning "river" and "pig") is also known as the pufferfish, blowfish or globefish, because it can puff itself up with water, to make it look bigger to its enemies in the sea.

● However, the fugu hardly needs to do the blowing up thing, because the fish also contains a **deadly poison**—another natural defence mechanism to ward off predators.

● The poison, **tetrododoxin,** is found in the skin, skeleton, ovaries, intestines and particularly the liver.

The food

● Fugu has long been a delicacy in Japan, and there are about 3800 fugu restaurants in the country today.

● Preparation is strictly controlled by law; fugu chefs must go through rigorous training for years to gain the certification that allows them to prepare the fish for human consumption. At the end of the training, there is a test in which the chef must prepare a fugu dish—and eat it!

● In restaurants, fugu is usually eaten raw, as sashimi, cut into very thin slices. Opinion is mixed about the taste; some say it's a bit like chicken, but it does have a delicate, gelatinous texture.

● If you want to order it yourself, make sure you see the chef's certificate before you commit! And if you aren't squeamish, read on to the next page.

There is evidence that the Egyptians knew about fugu poisoning. And the explorer James Cook described what some believe to be the deadly effect in his 1774 journal, after some crew members ate the fish.

The discarded organs and bones are placed in tightly sealed containers and taken away to be burned.

In Japan, the best time to eat fugu is in January and February.

The belly is covered with thousands of sharp, spiny quills.

The poison

● **If the fish is prepared properly, the flesh can be eaten safely.** It's even possible to eat parts of the organs if they are thoroughly washed out. Nevertheless, in Japan the most lethal part, the liver, cannot be sold, and the whole fish is banned in the European Union.

● Some people like to eat the fish with a tiny amount of toxin left in it. They feel a **tingling in the lips,** and it's this effect that attracts people. But it's a dangerous move, because if there is too much toxin, diners will soon experience something much worse.

● Tetrododoxin does not cross the blood-brain barrier, so the **victims remain fully conscious while their central nervous system gradually shuts down,** first producing dizziness and incoherent speech, then paralysing the muscles. This can lead to asphyxia, and possibly death. (There is no antidote for fugu poisoning.)

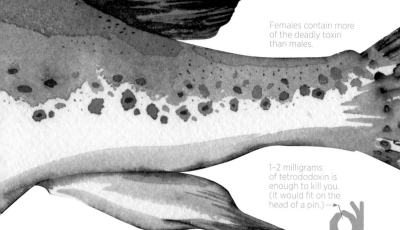

Females contain more of the deadly toxin than males.

1–2 milligrams of tetrodoxin is enough to kill you. (It would fit on the head of a pin.) →

And ...

● By restricting the fish's diet, some food companies are producing a **poison-free fugu** in aqua farms.

● As well as in Japanese restaurants, there are **other countries where you can eat fugu,** including the USA, and South Korea. (The fish itself is found in waters around the world.) The thrill of eating something that might kill you is clearly addictive.

● If you'd like a slightly **creepy Japanese souvenir,** lanterns are made from the cleaned skin of the fugu. You can also buy fugu-skin toys and waterproof wallets.

How to eat a lobster
It's messy. But plunge ahead anyway.

1 Twist off the claws.

2 Crack each claw with a nutcracker, pliers or hammer (or even a lobster claw cracker, if you have such a thing).

PINCHER CLAW

EYE

ANTENNULES

EYE

Although their eyes are prominent, lobsters are practically blind. But their short antennules sense distant odours carried by seawater, which helps them to find food, choose mates and decide if danger is near. The longer antennae are also sense organs.

ANTENNA

What do lobsters eat?

Mostly they eat other animals: crabs, mussels, clams, starfish, sea urchins and shrimp. They also eat parts of their old shells after moulting. (The calcium strengthens the new shell that's forming.)

CRUSHER CLAW

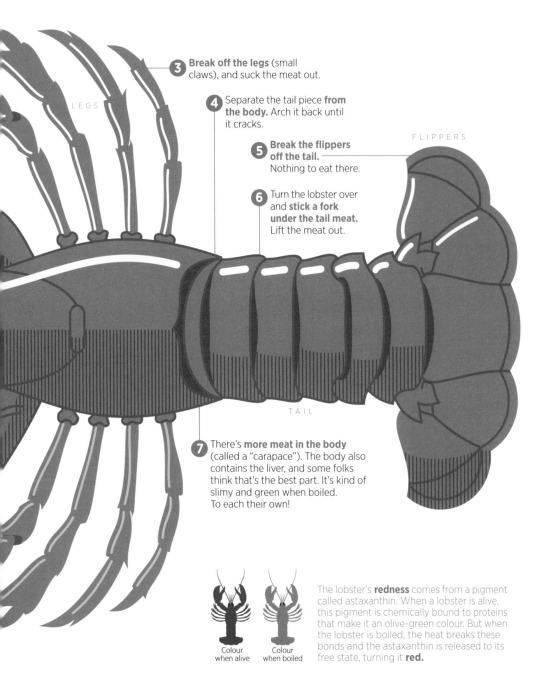

LEGS

FLIPPERS

3 **Break off the legs** (small claws), and suck the meat out.

4 Separate the tail piece **from the body.** Arch it back until it cracks.

5 **Break the flippers off the tail.** Nothing to eat there.

6 Turn the lobster over and **stick a fork under the tail meat.** Lift the meat out.

TAIL

7 There's **more meat in the body** (called a "carapace"). The body also contains the liver, and some folks think that's the best part. It's kind of slimy and green when boiled. To each their own!

Colour when alive   Colour when boiled

The lobster's **redness** comes from a pigment called astaxanthin. When a lobster is alive, this pigment is chemically bound to proteins that make it an olive-green colour. But when the lobster is boiled, the heat breaks these bonds and the astaxanthin is released to its free state, turning it **red.**

What to eat in the jungle

Some cultures eat insects and small animals as part of their daily diet; for others they are just a delicacy. For you, they might be all you can find.

Entomophagy is the word used by people who know about these things when they are talking about humans eating insects. (Animals that eat insects are called **insectivores.**)

You won't care about long words if you are hungry in the jungle or the bush, and you'll probably eat anything you can get your hands on.

Here are some dishes for your evening meal when you've run out of normal food.

Termites

You'll need to gather a great many of these tiny insects to make a meal. Some say they taste like peanut butter, others liken the taste to 10-day old curdled milk. But they are a good source of protein.

Frogs

This is the European edible frog (the kind French restaurants use when they serve frogs' legs), but there are many other frogs that you can eat. Skin all frogs before you cook them.

Beetle grubs

The white grubs of wood-infesting beetles are perfectly edible if you split their bodies and toast or fry them. You'll find them in decaying and rotten wood.

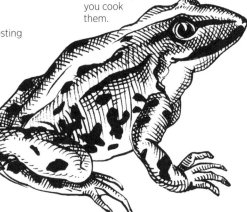

Birds

All birds are edible, but stay away from those that eat dead animals—vultures and kites—their flesh tastes terrible.

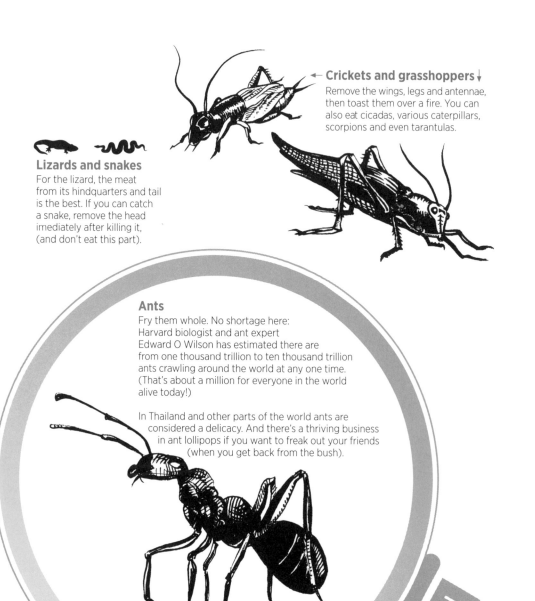

← Crickets and grasshoppers ↓

Remove the wings, legs and antennae, then toast them over a fire. You can also eat cicadas, various caterpillars, scorpions and even tarantulas.

Lizards and snakes

For the lizard, the meat from its hindquarters and tail is the best. If you can catch a snake, remove the head imediately after killing it, (and don't eat this part).

Ants

Fry them whole. No shortage here: Harvard biologist and ant expert Edward O Wilson has estimated there are from one thousand trillion to ten thousand trillion ants crawling around the world at any one time. (That's about a million for everyone in the world alive today!)

In Thailand and other parts of the world ants are considered a delicacy. And there's a thriving business in ant lollipops if you want to freak out your friends (when you get back from the bush).

Travel is like a box of chocolates ... you never know what you're gonna get

Well, that's not exactly what Tom Hanks said in the film *Forrest Gump,* but here's lots of stuff about that box of chocolates you are taking home as a present for Mum.

Chocolate milestones

500 Cocoa powder was in use by the Mayans (traces have been found in their pottery).

1502 On his fourth voyage to the Americas, Columbus found a stash of cocoa beans in what is now Honduras and sent some back to the King of Spain. Beans were used as currency by the Aztecs.

1525 Conquistador Hernán Cortés introduced cocoa to Charles V of Spain. The Aztecs mixed powdered beans with chili peppers to make a bitter **chocolate drink;** Europeans discovered they could add sugar and vanilla instead.

1756 The first chocolate factory is opened in Germany.

1828 In Holland, Conrad van Houten patented a hydraulic press that squeezed much of the fat from roasted beans, leaving a substance that could be ground into a fine powder—**cocoa.**

1849 In England, Joseph Fry produced the first solid **eating chocolate.**

1879 In Switzerland, Daniel Peter mixed cocoa powder with powdered milk (invented by Swiss chemist Henri Nestle) to make **milk chocolate.**

1907 Milton Hershey produced his first Kisses.

1937 The English company Rowntree introduced *Chocolate Niblet Beans.* In 1938, they were renamed *Smarties.* (In the USA, Forrest Mars Sr. copied this idea, in 1941, calling his product *M&Ms.*)

2003 Kathryn Ratcliffe ate 138 *Smarties* in 3 minutes using chopsticks, and entered the *Guinness Book of Records.*

How it's made

1 The cacao beans are taken out of the pods and left to **ferment,** reducing their bitterness.

2 The beans are **dried, cleaned, graded** and **shipped** to chocolate processing plants, where they are **roasted.**

3 The hard outer shells are removed, leaving kernels (called **nibs**).

4 A machine with revolving heated granite rollers (called a "melangeur") **mashes** the nibs into a thick paste, called "chocolate liquor".

The melangeur

Chocolate liquor is the base from which all chocolate products are made.

5 The paste is heated to ensure a smooth consistency, in a process known as **conching.**

6 The liquid chocolate is alternately heated and cooled for several hours. This **tempering** gives the final product its sheen and the familiar crack when you break it apart.

7 The liquid is **moulded** and **cooled** (to harden it), and then finally **packaged.**

Top cocoa-producing countries

millions of metric tons

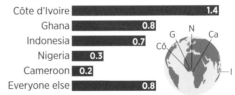

Côte d'Ivoire	1.4
Ghana	0.8
Indonesia	0.7
Nigeria	0.3
Cameroon	0.2
Everyone else	0.8

Where does the word "chocolate" come from?

Experts disagree, but it's probably from the Nahuatl* word *xocolatl*, which means "bitter water".

*A language indigenous to Central Mexico.

Spotty?

Academic institutions have done studies showing that eating chocolate does not cause acne.

Eating chocolate — Not eating chocolate

(Apparently the milk in milk chocolate has something to do with acne.)

Botany

The small cacao tree (*Theobroma cacao**) was originally found in the forests of Central and South America. It now grows in many countries 20 degrees above and below the equator.

The fruit of the cacao tree is a huge berry (or pod)—this is life-sized— that sprouts straight out of the branches and trunk of the tree.

There are 30 to 40 cacao beans inside each pod. It takes 10 pods to make 0.5kg (1lb) of cocoa.

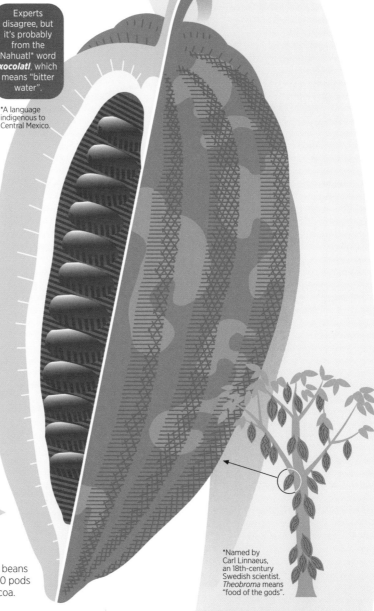

*Named by Carl Linnaeus, an 18th-century Swedish scientist. *Theobroma* means "food of the gods".

Beer is one of the oldest drinks produced by humans.
Chemical tests of jars from 3500 BCE found in modern-day Iran,
show traces of brewed ale. Over time, brewing has moved from those first artisinal efforts
through mass production starting in the Industrial Revolution, and
recently back to micro-breweries producing special ales and lagers.

Here's the basic brewing process

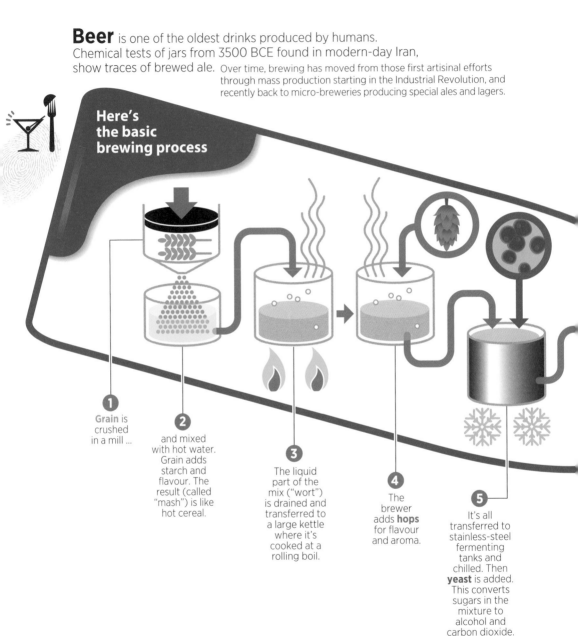

1 **Grain** is crushed in a mill ...

2 and mixed with hot water. Grain adds starch and flavour. The result (called "mash") is like hot cereal.

3 The liquid part of the mix ("wort") is drained and transferred to a large kettle where it's cooked at a rolling boil.

4 The brewer adds **hops** for flavour and aroma.

5 It's all transferred to stainless-steel fermenting tanks and chilled. Then **yeast** is added. This converts sugars in the mixture to alcohol and carbon dioxide.

The 10 b(eer)est countries

The amount of beer drunk per person there in 2016,* in **litres** (gallons)

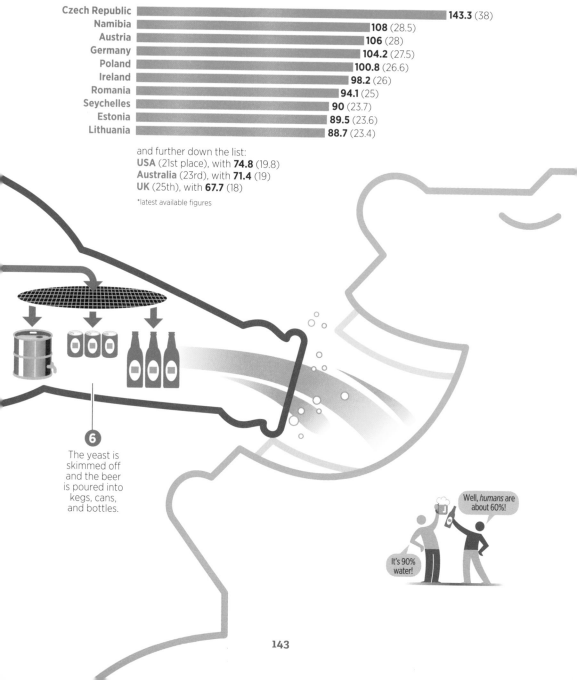

Czech Republic	**143.3** (38)
Namibia	**108** (28.5)
Austria	**106** (28)
Germany	**104.2** (27.5)
Poland	**100.8** (26.6)
Ireland	**98.2** (26)
Romania	**94.1** (25)
Seychelles	**90** (23.7)
Estonia	**89.5** (23.6)
Lithuania	**88.7** (23.4)

and further down the list:
USA (21st place), with **74.8** (19.8)
Australia (23rd), with **71.4** (19)
UK (25th), with **67.7** (18)

*latest available figures

6
The yeast is skimmed off and the beer is poured into kegs, cans, and bottles.

Well, *humans* are about 60%!

It's 90% water!

Making great crêpes

Let's start with a good recipe.

You'll need these ...

- 500ml (1pt) milk
- 3 eggs, beaten
- 1 cup of flour
- 1 1/2 teaspoons of sugar
- 1/8 teaspoon of salt
- 2 tablespoons of butter, melted

to make the batter

1. Put the flour in a bowl and make a well in the centre.

2. Add the milk slowly, whisking it in as you go.

3. Whisk in the beaten egg, then the butter.

4. Add the salt and sugar, whisk to combine.

Some fillings

- berries of all kinds
- apples
- peaches
- rhubarb
- bananas
- jam
- peanut butter
- mascarpone cheese
- sautéed vegetables
- roasted red peppers
- ... in fact almost anything sweet or savoury!

Now get crêping

5. Get a medium-sized pan nice and hot over high heat. Lightly grease with butter, then add enough of the batter to **thinly** cover the pan (crêpes must be thin). Tilt the pan to get an even spread, **cook for about a minute.** Flip it over for another minute and voila! Now repeat until you have a nice stack of crêpes ready to work with.

6. When you're ready to serve, place a crêpe into your warm, buttered pan and add your filling on one side. **Fold the crêpe in half** (over the filling), then into a quarter, if you like. Warm it gently and it's ready to eat. Get 'em while they're hot!

C'est magnifique!

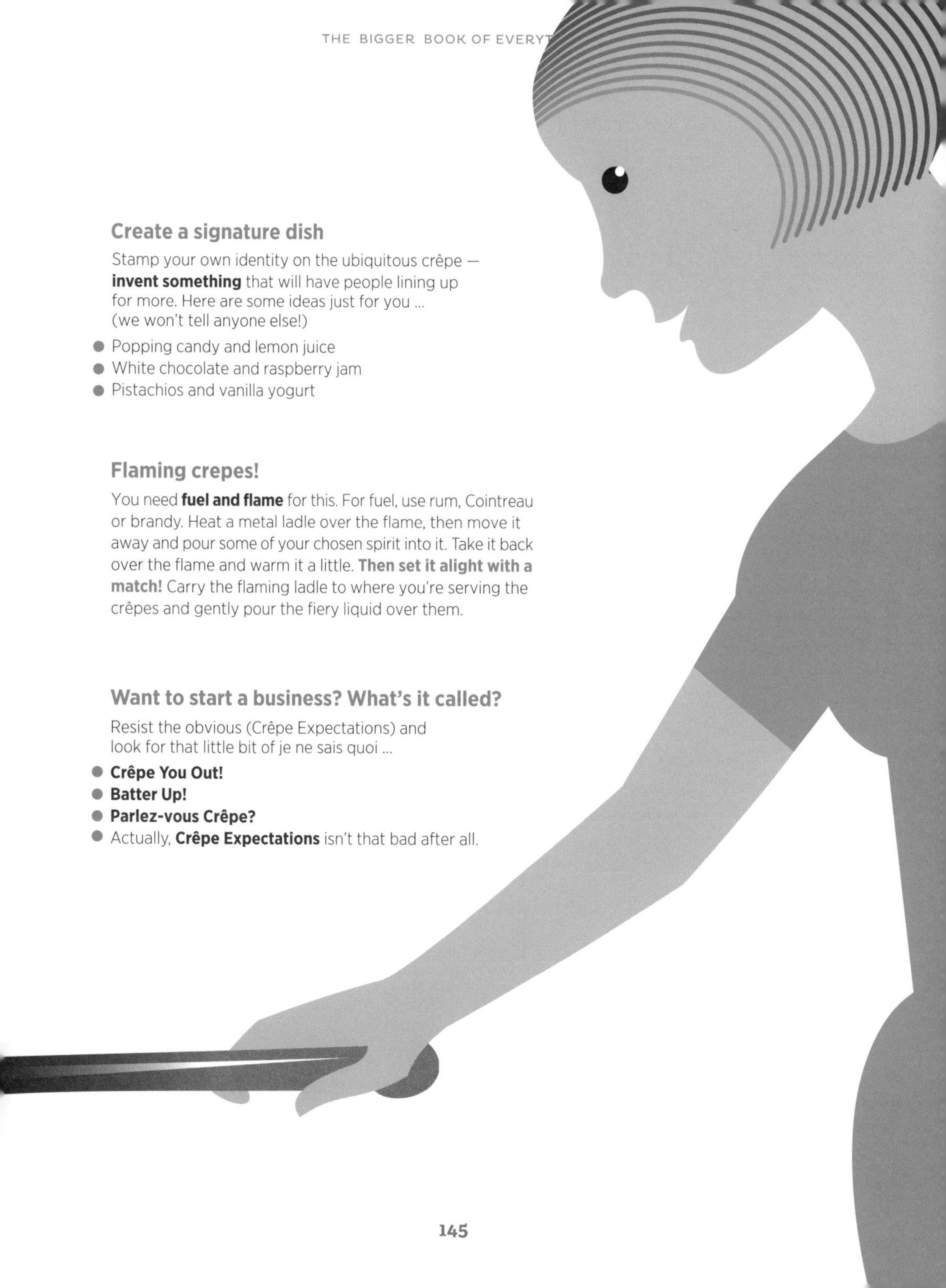

Create a signature dish

Stamp your own identity on the ubiquitous crêpe — **invent something** that will have people lining up for more. Here are some ideas just for you … (we won't tell anyone else!)

- Popping candy and lemon juice
- White chocolate and raspberry jam
- Pistachios and vanilla yogurt

Flaming crepes!

You need **fuel and flame** for this. For fuel, use rum, Cointreau or brandy. Heat a metal ladle over the flame, then move it away and pour some of your chosen spirit into it. Take it back over the flame and warm it a little. **Then set it alight with a match!** Carry the flaming ladle to where you're serving the crêpes and gently pour the fiery liquid over them.

Want to start a business? What's it called?

Resist the obvious (Crêpe Expectations) and look for that little bit of je ne sais quoi …

- **Crêpe You Out!**
- **Batter Up!**
- **Parlez-vous Crêpe?**
- Actually, **Crêpe Expectations** isn't that bad after all.

JAPANESE tea time

The essence of the Japanese tea ceremony is to convey grace, harmony and respect.

1. The tea master enters the ceremony room and bows.

2. The ceremony begins with ritual cleansing of utensils.

3. Matcha green tea powder (three scoops for each guest) is spooned into the tea bowl with the chashuku.

4. The tea master ladles hot water into the tea bowl.

5. He stirs it with the chasen into a paste, and will add more water as necessary to make it into a soup-like consistency.

6. The tea is inspected before being offered to the guest.

Tea ceremony utensils

KAMA cast-iron kettle

CHASHUKU tea ladle

CHAWAN tea bowl

CHASEN tea whisk

和

Essential to tea ceremonies are **hanging scrolls,** which display words such as *Respect, Purity, Tranquility,* and, as here, ← *Harmony.*

7 The guest takes the tea, bows and returns to a position on the floor.

8 The tea is swallowed in one go.

9 Etiquette dictates that the guest should admire the bowl and ask about its provenance.

☕ A double* cappucino, please!

The barista in your local coffee shop will make it just for you. Did you know that **bar** is the pressure rating on most espresso machines that baristas use (usually it's 135 lb/sq in)? But that isn't where the word barista comes from — it means bartender in Italian.

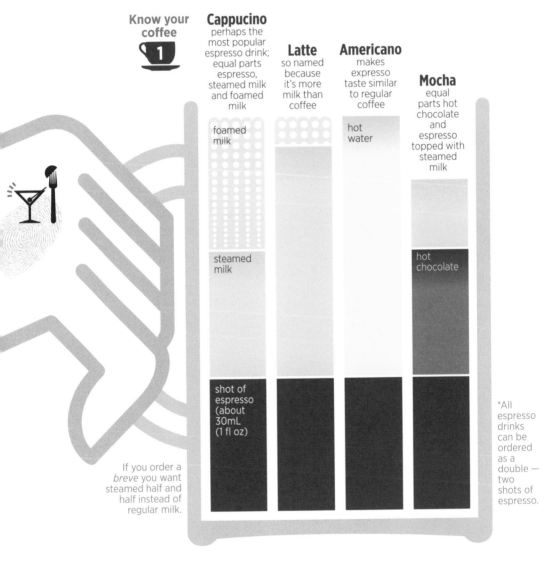

Know your coffee

1

Cappucino
perhaps the most popular espresso drink; equal parts espresso, steamed milk and foamed milk

Latte
so named because it's more milk than coffee

Americano
makes expresso taste similar to regular coffee

Mocha
equal parts hot chocolate and espresso topped with steamed milk

foamed milk

hot water

steamed milk

hot chocolate

shot of espresso (about 30mL (1 fl oz)

If you order a *breve* you want steamed half and half instead of regular milk.

*All espresso drinks can be ordered as a double — two shots of espresso.

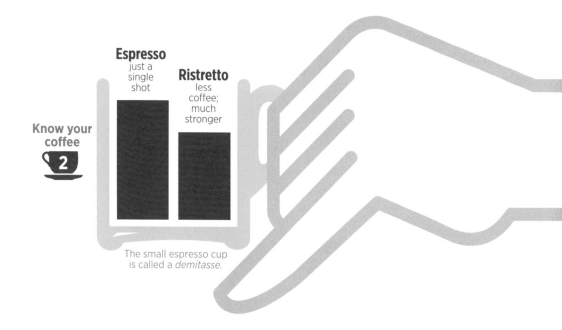

Espresso
just a
single
shot

Ristretto
less
coffee;
much
stronger

**Know your
coffee**

The small espresso cup
is called a *demitasse*.

Making coffee without going out for it

You can buy fairly decent, small versions of the professional espresso machines you see in coffee shops, but here are some other ways to be your own barista.

Stove-top espresso

Water is boiled in the lower part, forced up a tube then it flows down through finely ground beans.

Filter

Finely ground beans are placed into a paper or reusable plastic cone, and boiling water poured over it. While grounds stay in the cone, the coffee is ready to drink.

Plunger

Boiling water is poured over coarsely ground beans. After a few minutes, the plunger is pushed to the bottom of the pot, trapping the grounds while you pour the coffee.

Percolator

Credited with civilising America's Wild West, a coffee percolator boils water, sending it up through a tube and down over coarsely ground beans held in a metal filter at the top.

How to make sushi

Sushi was first eaten in Japan in the 8th century. At first it was a way to preserve fish in fermented rice. Later, people started eating the rice as well. In the 19th century, sushi became the original fast food. Here's how to roll one like an expert.

1 **Make sushi rice.**

● Wash the short grain or "sushi" rice. It can be white or brown.

● Cover rice with water and bring to boil, then turn heat down and cover. Cook for 6 to 8 minutes.

● While it's cooking, heat rice vinegar, sugar and salt until the sugar dissolves.

● Put cooked rice in a large bowl; add vinegar mixture and fold together.

● To keep the texture, use soon. Don't refrigerate, it will harden the rice.

2 Use a **bamboo sushi-rolling mat.**

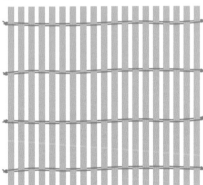

3 Add a **sheet of nori,** rough side up. Then put a handful of rice on top ...

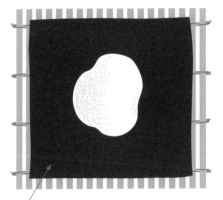

Nori is thin, paper-thin, dried seaweed that holds the sushi rice and filling together when rolled up.

4 and **spread it evenly,** 1.25cm (0.5in) thick. Leave 2.5cm (1in) all round.

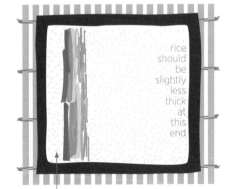

rice should be slightly less thick at this end

5 Add strips of fish and vegetables (or just veggies) starting a little way in from this edge.

6 **Roll up tightly,** squeezing as you go.

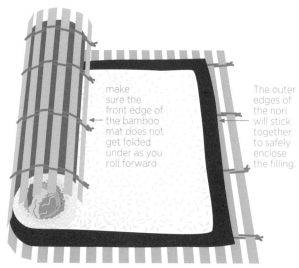

make sure the front edge of the bamboo mat does not get folded under as you roll forward

The outer edges of the nori will stick together to safely enclose the filling.

7 **Cut** into 2.5cm (1in) pieces.

Sushi rolls are called maki. They can also be made with the rice on the outside—the nori just holds the filling together.

8 **Serve** with soy sauce for dipping and pickled ginger as a palate cleanser (don't put it on the sushi).

Beware of sushi snobs who say no to table-side soy sauce. What they mean is that sushi chefs add rice vinegar to the rice, so you may not need any extra seasoning. It's up to you.

Inside story

You can put almost anything into a roll. Here are some traditional choices:

sliced vegetables
carrots
cucumber
scallions
avocado
spicy pickles
cooked spinach
shiitake mushrooms
sweet potato

raw fish
tuna
salmon

cooked fish
sliced tuna steaks
shrimp
crabmeat

Translating the the menu when you decide to go out and let someone else make the sushi

shake	fresh salmon
maguro	bluefin tuna
hamachi	yellowfin tuna
toro	fatty tuna
ebi	cooked shrimp
unagi	grilled freshwater eel
tai	red snapper
kani	crabmeat
tamago	sweet egg custard wrapped in dried seaweed
tempura	fish or veggies dipped in batter and deep fried
uni	sea urchin
wasabi	Japanese horseradish

Say cheese

Cheesemaking is not that complicated; it's all in the details—details that can produce a huge variety of tastes (and smells!). Estimates vary for how many different cheeses there are in the world, ranging from 500 to 1,000.

Let's look at just one of them: **cheddar.**

The milk

● There are two main breeds of milking cow. Many cheesemakers like **Brown Swiss** cows ( ) because they produce protein-rich milk, and they continue to produce it for longer than the average **Holstein** — the classic picture-book cow ( ).

● **The quality of the milk depends on what the cows eat.** Fresh pasture with a mixture of grasses and legumes is best. Here are three **legumes** that the Brown Swiss love:

clover

alfafa

timothy

The process

1 **Raw milk** is piped into a huge stainless steel vat.

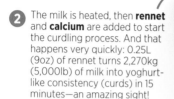

2 The milk is heated, then **rennet** and **calcium** are added to start the curdling process. And that happens very quickly: 0.25L (9oz) of rennet turns 2,270kg (5,000lb) of milk into yoghurt-like consistency (curds) in 15 minutes—an amazing sight!

3 The **curds** are sliced into tiny cubes.

4 A **mechanical stirrer** separates the semi-solid curds from the liquid whey, which is drained off.

5 The whey is reconstituted into **whey protein** and sold for livestock feed, or spread onto the cows' pasture.

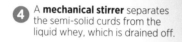

6 **Salt** is added, then the curds are stacked to drain further and clump together. This process is called **cheddaring.**

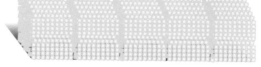

7 Next, the cheese is **pressed** into various sizes; some become large round wheels, others, rectangular blocks. (See cheese rolling in a couple of pages.)

8 Finally, it's **aged** from three months to two years. Longer aging produces a sharper-tasting cheese.

Next: **production and addiction**→

What's the cheesemaker's motto? Tell me. "No whey."

Cheesy animals

It's not just cows, of course.

From cows and goats
you get

kilogram
(2.2lb)
of cheese

from every

10

litres
(2.6gal)
of milk.

From sheep
you get

kilogram
(2.2lb)
of cheese

from every

6

litres
(1.6gal)
of milk.

This means that sheep's milk cheese is much richer.

Camel's milk
is made into cheese In dry desert areas of Africa and the Middle East. The milk has enough nutrients to sustain a person throughout the day.

This milk is good for people with lactose intolerance, and has lower cholesterol than other animals' milk.

They make cheese from camel's milk in Mauritania. They call it Camelbert.

Why we ♥ cheese
Don't worry, you can't help it.

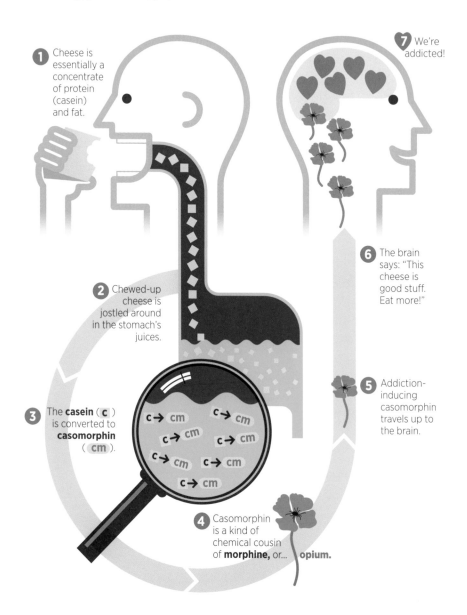

1 Cheese is essentially a concentrate of protein (casein) and fat.

2 Chewed-up cheese is jostled around in the stomach's juices.

3 The **casein** (**c**) is converted to **casomorphin** (**cm**).

4 Casomorphin is a kind of chemical cousin of **morphine,** or... **opium.**

5 Addiction-inducing casomorphin travels up to the brain.

6 The brain says: "This cheese is good stuff. Eat more!"

7 We're addicted!

Bitters: essential again

Once widely used by bartenders, bitters fell out of fashion. With the return to a new era of cocktails, bitters are becoming a new staple in bars, incorporated again in classic drinks as well as new concoctions.

1 shot = 30mL (1oz)

The daddy of all bitters is Angostura, still sold with its original 100-year-old paper label.

Other bitters include:
Regans' Orange Bitters
Peychaud's Bitters
The Bitter Truth
Fee Brothers Bitters

Usually you only need a dash—a mere drop or two, although the recipes shown here suggest more. (Like all recipes, adjust quantities to suit your taste.)

These drinks are adapted from a book entirely about bitters, appropriately titled *Bitters*, by Brad Thomas Parsons.

PINK GIN

Very simple. A navy favourite starting in the 19th century (perhaps because it was recommended for seasickness).

> 2 shots gin
> 4–6 dashes Angostura Bitters

Chill the coupe glass first.

CHAMPAGNE COCKTAIL

Put the sugar cube into the coupe glass (or flute) and soak with the bitters. Fill the glass with chilled champagne.

> 1 sugar cube
> 4–6 dashes Angostura Bitters
> Champagne
> lemon

CRICKET BALL

Drop the sugar cube into the flute, Soak with both the bitters. Add the Lillet. Fill up with prosecco.

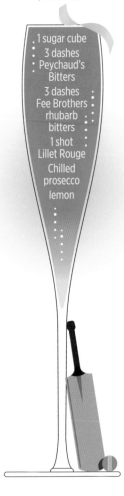

> 1 sugar cube
> 3 dashes Peychaud's Bitters
> 3 dashes Fee Brothers rhubarb bitters
> 1 shot Lillet Rouge
> Chilled prosecco
> lemon

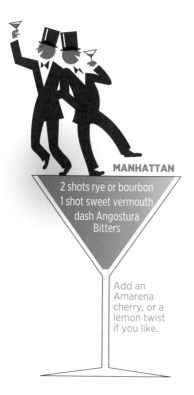

MANHATTAN

2 shots rye or bourbon
1 shot sweet vermouth
dash Angostura
Bitters

Add an
Amarena
cherry, or a
lemon twist
if you like.

OLD-FASHIONED

Some folks muddle fruit in the glass
before adding the alcohol. Here's the
original recipe; it's perfect with a
simple lemon twist.

2 shots rye or bourbon
1/4 shot simple syrup
3 dashes Angostura Bitters
lemon twist

Simple syrup: heat one cup of sugar and one
of water until sugar is dissolved. Just before it
boils, turn off the heat, and allow to cool.

No bitters in this one—just a great way to impress your guests!

The amazing
POUSSE CAFÉ

This works on the principle that
some liquids are more dense than
others. Thicker, heavier liquids go
in first, and each succeeding
one floats on top of the
one before it.

Pour each liquid slowly over
a teaspoon held bottom side up
and just touching the inside of
the glass.

1/2 shot
brandy

1/2 shot
green Chartreuse

1/2 shot
crème de cassis

1/2 shot white
crème de cacao

1/2 shot
yellow Chartreuse

1/2 shot
Grenadine

If the layers don't
quite sit properly,
leave the drink for
ten minutes; it will
eventually settle
back into stripes.

Sip one
layer at
a time.

Cook like a Maori

The traditional Maori way to cook food is in a hangi. In New Zealand nowadays it's typically reserved for special occasions, but the method shown here goes back at least two thousand years, and it's still used in Chile and parts of Africa.

Here's what you'll need

- large stones
- 1 cubic metre of firewood
- kindling (to get it started)
- meat
- vegetables
- chickenwire baskets (the kids can make these; you'll need chickenwire, pliers ... and sticking-plasters)
- cloths, sheets, hessian sacks
- large bucket of water
- shovels, rakes
- heavy duty gloves (to protect hands while lifting the wire baskets out of the pit)
- strong friends to help dig the hole
- beer (lots)

The whole thing takes about six hours, so **LET'S GET GOING!**

1 BUILD A FIRE

Cover an area 1m (about 3ft) square with large river stones. Make sure you are about 3m (nearly 10ft) from any structure, foliage, drains or septic tanks.

Place kindling, then a stack of logs on top of the stones and light the fire. Keep feeding the pile of wood for **two to three hours** so that the stones get white hot.

Stones can explode when heated, so it's a good idea to do a test run—heat them up—24 hours before the event to make sure you're using the right type of stones.

(You can use iron bars instead of stones; you'll need to get these red hot.)

It's thirsty work. Have a beer. Or two.

2 DIG A PIT

While the stones are heating up, dig a hole **1m (3ft) deep and 1m square,** near the fire.

3 MAKE THE WIRE BASKETS

This'll keep the young ones busy while you are digging. The aim is just to contain the food when it's in the pit; so the baskets can be very simply constructed.

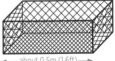

← about 0.5m (1.6ft) →

4 PREPARE THE FOOD

Wrap the meat and veggies in old, wet tea towels or other clean cloths, and place them in the wire baskets.

Put the meat and veggies in separate cloths.

You might want to line the baskets with tinfoil; this will ensure none of the earth or ash from the pit gets mixed up with the food.

⑤ HOT STONES INTO THE PIT

When the stones, or iron bars are hot—that'll take two hours or a bit more with the fire on top of them—pull the wood aside, and drag the stones or bars into the pit with rakes. (Leave them in the fire longer if they aren't *really, really* hot.)

This would not be a good time to fall into the pit.

⑥ START COOKING

So as not to lose heat, put the wire baskets with the bundles of food inside into the pit as quickly as you can. The meat-filled baskets should go in first, then the vegetables.

top layer: veg
bottom: meat

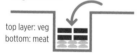

⑦ COVER THE FOOD

Lay old sheets on top of the baskets, then the hessian sacks.

sacks
sheets

⑧ POUR WATER ON IT

A large bucketful.

⑨ STEAM!

Pouring water on the hot stones will produce **a lot** of steam. ┈┈┈┈┈┈┈┈┈┈┈┈► **Caution:** if you get burned by the steam, flush the wound with cold water.

Quickly shovel the pile of earth from the pit back into it to trap as much of the steam as possible. No-one wants half-cooked meat.

⑩ WAIT

Could it possibly be time for another...?

Cheers! When do we eat?

Here's to the hangi!

⑪ THREE HOURS LATER...

Dig the whole thing up. Take care not to stick your shovel into the wire baskets.

⑫ FINALLY! UNWRAP AND EAT

If you've timed it right, by now the sun is probably setting, so no-one can tell if some of the food is a bit raw anyway. And, you guessed, beer goes really well with it.

POSTSCRIPT

Once dark, it's traditional for a few people to stumble into the pit. Please leave the sacks and cloths on the now-cold stones to break their fall.

Keeping bees

Bees pollinate 80% of flowering crops, and that's about one-third of everything we eat. But bees are under attack by Colony Collapse Disorder, a disease that's reducing bee populations around the world.

So beekeeping is important. (Of course it is!—why do you think I'm in this book?)
Here's how to get going:

1 FIND A COURSE TO TAKE
Colleges and universities that specialise in agriculture are a good place to start: they'll have links to further education courses and local beekeepers and beekeeping clubs.

2 DO RESEARCH
There are lots of books about beekeeping. You can also search the web for information.

3 BUY OR BUILD A HIVE
Lots of parts!

Waterproof outer cover

Inner cover

"Super" (more of these can be added)
Worker bees make honey here

Queen excluder
Worker bees can pass through

Brood chamber
Queen lays eggs here

Entrance block (for bees)

Hive stand

Old-fashioned hives (called "skeps") were made of straw.

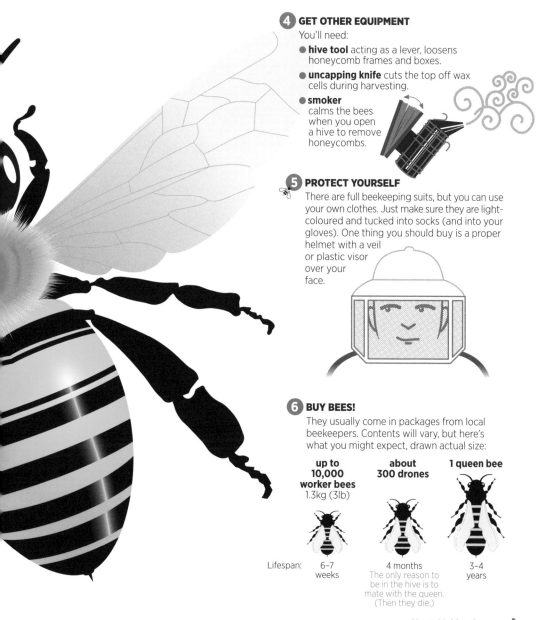

4 GET OTHER EQUIPMENT

You'll need:

- **hive tool** acting as a lever, loosens honeycomb frames and boxes.
- **uncapping knife** cuts the top off wax cells during harvesting.
- **smoker** calms the bees when you open a hive to remove honeycombs.

5 PROTECT YOURSELF

There are full beekeeping suits, but you can use your own clothes. Just make sure they are light-coloured and tucked into socks (and into your gloves). One thing you should buy is a proper helmet with a veil or plastic visor over your face.

6 BUY BEES!

They usually come in packages from local beekeepers. Contents will vary, but here's what you might expect, drawn actual size:

up to 10,000 worker bees 1.3kg (3lb)	**about 300 drones**	**1 queen bee**
Lifespan: 6–7 weeks	4 months The only reason to be in the hive is to mate with the queen. (Then they die.)	3–4 years

Next: Making honey →

Making honey

Not to put too fine a point on it, but honey starts out as bee-vomit.

1 COLLECTING NECTAR

Forager bees collect nectar from flowering plants.

Forager bees regurgitate nectar into **processor bees.**

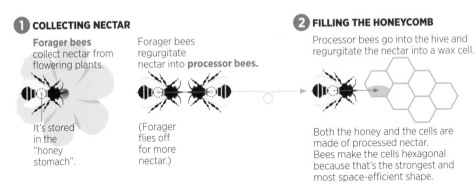

It's stored in the "honey stomach".

(Forager flies off for more nectar.)

2 FILLING THE HONEYCOMB

Processor bees go into the hive and regurgitate the nectar into a wax cell.

Both the honey and the cells are made of processed nectar. Bees make the cells hexagonal because that's the strongest and most space-efficient shape.

3 DRYING THE NECTAR

Honey is about 18% water but nectar is 70%, so bees must dry it out by fanning their wings to create an airflow around the honeycomb.

70%

18%

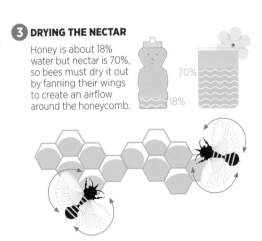

4 CAPPING THE CELLS

When the nectar in the cells has ripened and evaporated, it becomes thick, sweet honey. Bees then cap the cells with more of the nectar from their stomachs, and it hardens into wax.

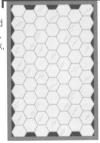

5 HARVESTING THE HONEY: 1

You don't have to destroy the honeycomb to gather honey. (This is a big relief to the bees who spent many hours making it.) First you must scrape off the outer wax coating (see 4) with the uncapping knife.

Some knives have electric heating coils.

6 HARVESTING: 2

Scraped honeycomb frames are placed in a centrifuge machine which spins the honey out of the cells. The comb is returned to the hive and the bees get to work again.

What to do if you get stung (and you probably will)

- Pull the stinger out.
- Take an ibuprofen or acetaminophen tablet to relieve the pain.
- Wash with soap and water.
- Hold an ice-pack to the site for about 20 minutes. Relief should last for about 5 hours; re-ice if the pain comes back.
- Other home remedies include damp pastes of baking soda, toothpaste, raw onion or potato; calamine lotion; hydrocortisone cream; deodorant; even honey!
- **IMPORTANT:** If you start to have an allergic reaction, seek medical help immediately.

Not all bees sting—just females, and they usually die afer the deed—but they'll only attack you if threatened. This is why you need a smoker when moving parts of the hive.

What's on the menu?

Bees visit whatever flowers they can find and then naturally blend the gathered pollen and nectar. **Try these in your garden:**

- **Spring:** crocus, hyacinth, borage, calendula, wild lilac
- **Summer:** cosmos, echinacea, snapdragons, foxgloves, hosta
- **Late summer:** zinnias, sedum, asters, witch hazel, goldenrod

What else do bees pollinate? (Told you they were important!)

Apart from bees, other insects, birds, rain and wind are all pollinators, but bees are the most important. Here are the percentages of some of the crops pollinated by bees.

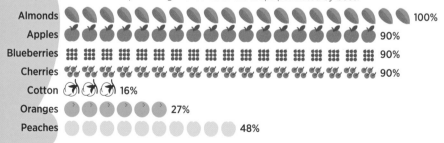

Almonds 100%
Apples 90%
Blueberries 90%
Cherries 90%
Cotton 16%
Oranges 27%
Peaches 48%

Tapping for maple syrup

In Canada, they tap telephone poles for sap (just kidding; old joke) but in Vermont, USA, getting sap out of maple trees is big business. It's hard work, in a cold climate.

1 In summer, the leaves of **sugar maple trees*** absorb sunlight and carbon dioxide, eventually converting them into sucrose. This is dissolved in the sap, and in the fall it's stored as starch in the roots.

Noisy crows herald the start of sugaring.

*You can tap silver, black and red maples as well as sugar maples. Other trees, such as birches and walnuts, yield some sap. Maples are the way to go.

2 In late winter, the cycle of freezing nights and 5°C (41°F) days creates pressure in the tree. This starts the sap flowing to the trunk from the branches and roots.

3 You drill 1cm (7/16in) holes into the trunk to a depth of about 7.5cm (3in) and tap the spouts in. Trees with a 25 cm (10in) diameter typically get one spout; those with 62 cm (24.5in) diameters get up to four spouts.

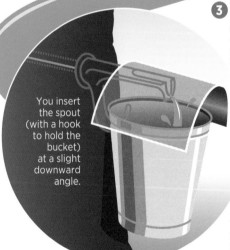

You insert the spout (with a hook to hold the bucket) at a slight downward angle.

The sap flows for between four to six weeks.

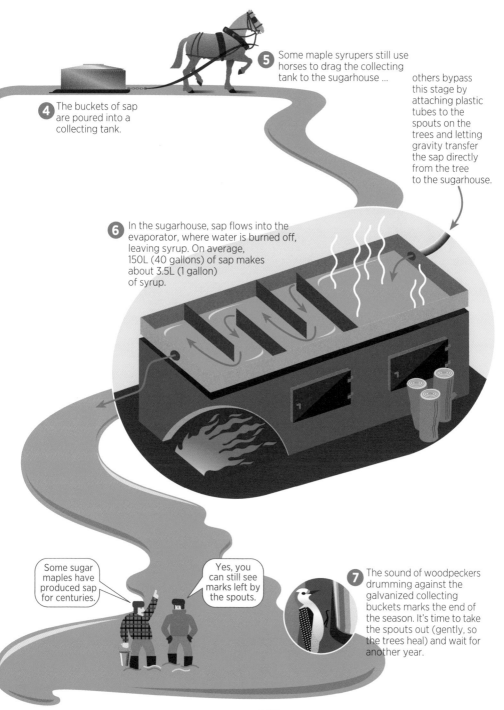

5 Some maple syrupers still use horses to drag the collecting tank to the sugarhouse ... others bypass this stage by attaching plastic tubes to the spouts on the trees and letting gravity transfer the sap directly from the tree to the sugarhouse.

4 The buckets of sap are poured into a collecting tank.

6 In the sugarhouse, sap flows into the evaporator, where water is burned off, leaving syrup. On average, 150L (40 gallons) of sap makes about 3.5L (1 gallon) of syrup.

Some sugar maples have produced sap for centuries.

Yes, you can still see marks left by the spouts.

7 The sound of woodpeckers drumming against the galvanized collecting buckets marks the end of the season. It's time to take the spouts out (gently, so the trees heal) and wait for another year.

HEALTH & SAFETY

AARRGHH! My back's killing me!

You do know that travelling can be exhausting, don't you? Sooner or later you'll overdo it, and often the first thing to give you trouble is your back. No gym or fitness centre is needed for these simple exercises.

Do them gently at first. If you continue with them regularly (even when there's no pain) you'll strengthen the muscles in your back, and there'll be less chance you'll have back problems on future trips.

1 Stand against a wall with your feet slightly forward.

2 Slide down (and back up) slowly.

Repeat a few times.

1 Sit up straight.

2 Reach as far as you can.

1 Kneel on floor.

2 Stretch forward and back with opposite arm and leg.

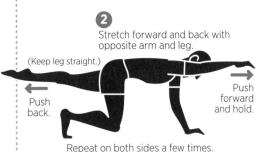

(Keep leg straight.)

Push back.

Push forward and hold.

Repeat on both sides a few times.

1 Lie on your back with knees bent; raise torso.

2 Bring knee to opposite elbow.

Repeat on both sides, in a continuous back-and-forth flow.

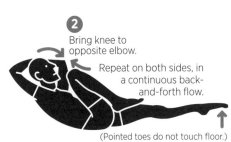

(Pointed toes do not touch floor.)

1 Lie flat on tummy and raise torso.

2 Raise whole body to "plank" position off the floor. Hold for a few seconds and repeat.

(Keep legs straight.)

How to carry an injured friend from a remote location

Accidents will happen. Here are five ways to transport the patient safely.

But if the injury has knocked the person out so they cannot be carried by one of these methods, you can make a pretty good stretcher out of blankets and strong sticks.

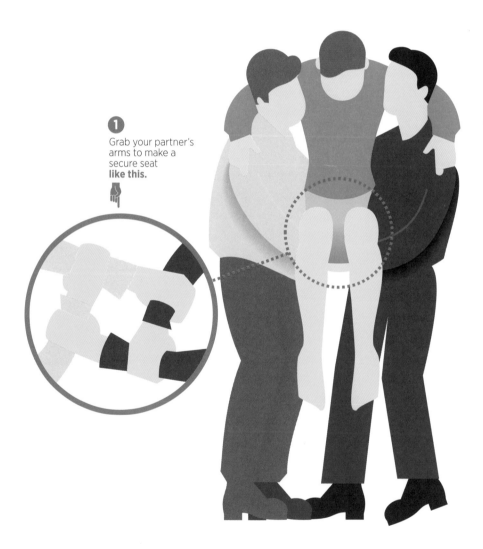

1 Grab your partner's arms to make a secure seat **like this.**

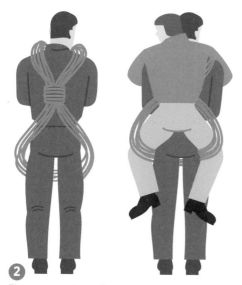

2 Tie your ropes into a figure eight.

3 If it's a long walk back to base, cut the bottom out of your backpack. It makes a workable adult version of a baby sling.

4 Slot a strong walking stick or thin branch through your backpack straps to make a seat.

5 Try the classic fireman's lift.

Vitaminology *(if that's a word)*

You should be getting all the vitamins your body needs by eating a balanced diet. But when you are travelling that can be difficult. Check out what you might be missing.

year discovered **1913**

generic name (letter) **A**

chemical name **retinol**

lack can lead to night blindness, eye disorders

good sources orange and yellow fruits, leafy vegetables, carrots, pumpkin, squash, spinach, liver, cod liver oil

1931 B5

pantothenic acid

paresthesia (skin numbness)

meat, broccoli, avocados, whole grains

1934 B6

pyridoxine

anaemia (blood disorders, fatigue)

meat, vegetables, tree nuts, bananas, dairy products

1931 B7

biotin

dermatitis (eczema)

raw egg yolk, peanuts, liver

1920 D

calciferol (D2); cholecalciferol (D3)

rickets (softening of bones)

fish, eggs, mushrooms, milk, liver, cod liver oil, sunshine

1922 E

≡ deficiency very rare ≡

tocopherol

poor blood cell and tissue heath

unrefined vegetable oils, wheat germ oil

1929 K

phylloquinone (K1); menaquinone (K2)

bleeding diathesis (susceptibility to bleeding)

leafy green vegetables, egg yolks, liver

1910

B₁

thiamine

beriberi (fatigue)

pork, oatmeal, brown rice, bran, vegetables, liver, eggs

1920

B₂

riboflavin

ariboflavinosis (sore throat, mouth swelling, cracked lips)

dairy products, bananas, popcorn, green beans, asparagus

1936

B₃

niacin

pellagra (sensitivity to sun, dermatitis, dementia, skin lesions)

meat, fish, eggs, mushrooms, tree nuts

1941

B₉

folic acid

megaloblast (birth defects during pregnancy)

leafy vegetables, pasta, bread, cereal, liver

1926

B₁₂

cobalamin

megaloblastic anaemia (blood disorders)

meat, eggs

1920

C

ascorbic acid

scurvy (lethargy, bone pain, easy bruising)

citrus and other fruit, vegetables, liver

Since **liver** seems to be the winning vitaminizer *(another new word?),* it seems right to give you a recipe for it:

● Calf's liver is best. Peel off the membrane, and cut into quarter-inch slices.

● Season with salt and pepper; coat with flour.

● Heat 2 tablespoons of vegetable oil or butter in a skillet over medium-high heat.

● Brown the liver quickly on both sides (only about 1–2 minutes; overcooking will turn it to leather!).

medium-high

1–2 minutes

Liver is good with onions. Slice them thinly; cook over low heat until soft (20+ minutes).

CPR: **we should all know how to do this**

→ **Cardio-**
→ **Pulmonary**
→ **Resuscitation**

= reviving
the heart
and lungs

1 **Call emergency services.**

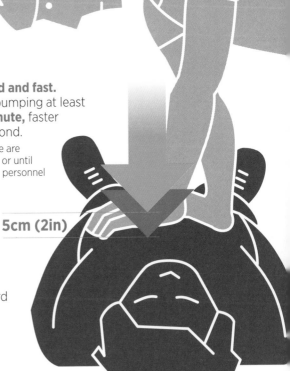

2 If the victim is not
breathing normally,
nor coughing
or moving,
**start chest
pumping.**

Push down,
in the centre
of the chest
**5cm (2in),
30 times.**

Keep going **hard and fast.**
You should be pumping at least
100 times a minute, faster
than once a second.

(Continue until there are
signs of movement, or until
emergency medical personnel
take over.)

This might seem
like a lot. You
may actually break
ribs doing this. But
remember, you are
saving a life here;
ribs can be mended,
death cannot.

5cm (2in)

Continuous, hard
chest pumping
is considered
to be the most
important part
of CPR.

Recently, health experts found that many people were not engaging in **mouth-to-mouth resuscitation** for fear of disease, or just because they were squeamish about doing it. Unfortunately, they also found that most people doing CPR were not pumping the chest hard or long enough. Therefore, CPR guidelines now place less emphasis on mouth-to-mouth, and more on pumping.

In fact, it is highly unlikely that you will get a disease from performing mouth-to-mouth, and filling the lungs up with air is important. So here's what you do:

3 Tilt the victim's head back
and listen for possible sounds of coughing or vomiting. (One result of pumping the chest is that the victim vomits. Turn the head to the side, and try to wipe the liquid out of the way.)

4 Pinch the nose and cover the mouth with yours. **Blow** in until you see the chest rise. Do this **twice.**

5 Repeat 30 pumps and two breaths until help comes.

6 Two people giving CPR is good: one pumping, one blowing air in. (Take turns, do not do both at once.)

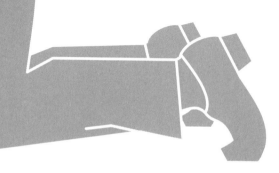

Beating jetlag

The tiredness you feel is your body's reaction to crossing time zones.
(A contributing factor is the stress of travelling in general.)
What you need to do is **reset your internal clock.**

BEFORE YOU GO

1 Try to **shift your sleep pattern.** Go to bed one hour earlier or later depending on which direction you are flying—but no more than 1 hour per night—for as many time zones as you are going to cross (or as many as you can manage).

2 If you are going on a really long flight (for instance, from Europe to Australia) take **melatonin** for 2-3 days before the trip.
For shorter trips, don't take it before you go. See "When you arrive" for when to use it.

Melatonin is a sleep-inducing hormone that occurs naturally in your brain and it controls the body's daily rhythm. It is available up to 3mg, but a lower dose (0.5mg) has been found to have the same effect. So less is better.

3 **Ginger tea** is thought to be a good way to counteract jetlag.

Here's a quick recipe:

● Boil water.
● Grate 2 teaspoons of fresh ginger (*much* better than powdered ginger) into a cup.
● Add boiling water.
● Allow to steep for 5 minutes.

Ideally you should drink it at the start of your trip, an hour before you take off, but often that's not possible. Instead, you might take a small piece of fresh ginger to **chew** on the plane—but beware, it's hot and spicy!

Jetlag is less pronounced when you travel **west,** and gain hours.

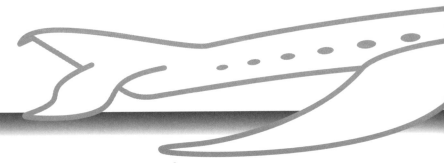

ON THE PLANE

1 **Go to sleep** as soon as possible. Wear loose clothing, a mask and earplugs.

2 **Don't take sleeping pills.** They will interfere with your sleep pattern when you arrive at your destination.

3 **Don't drink alcohol or coffee.** They dehydrate you and that emphasises the effects of jetlag, because your body is stressed by being dried out. Just drink water.

Jetlag is worse when you travel **east,** and lose hours.

WHEN YOU ARRIVE

1 Flying east or west, **stay up until it's bedtime** wherever you are.

2 **Walk around** in the sun. Here's hoping you are not in England in the winter or Seattle, USA, at any time. (Just kidding, Seattle.) If you must nap, make it for no more than an hour.

3 If you flew eastward, take a low dose of **melatonin** for 3 nights before bed.

If you flew westward, and find yourself waking up early the first morning there, take a low dose of melatonin.

In general, the time it takes for your body to adjust is **1 day for every time zone** you've crossed. You may not have time for that!

Travelling exercises

How to keep in shape while you're waiting for a plane, and when you're on board (or in a car, or a train).

BACK EXTENSIONS WHILE STANDING ...

Place both hands on your back at waist level. With your chin tucked in, slowly arch your upper body backwards and hold the position. Slowly straighten your back into an upright position. Relax and repeat.

LEG STRETCHES

While sitting, interlock the fingers of both hands and grasp your shin just below the knee. Then slowly pull the leg toward your chest. Hold. Repeat with your other leg.

AND SEATED

Position your hands on your back at the waist. Arch your upper body backward while tucking in your chin. Hold and repeat.

MORE LEG STRETCHES

Place one foot in front of the other and bend the forward knee while keeping the other leg straight. Lean forward and hold. Repeat with your other leg.

HEEL LIFT

Lift one heel as high as possible, but keep toes on the floor. Repeat with other foot.

FOOT FLEX

Lift toes up as far as you can, but keep heels on the floor. Relax and repeat.

SHOULDER ROLLS

Holding your arms at your side, slowly roll your shoulders both forward and backwards in wide circular motions. Repeat.

EYE ROTATIONS

Move your eyes slowly in all directions: clockwise, anticlockwise, side to side and up and down.

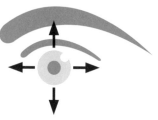

SHOULDER STRETCHES

Place right hand on your left shoulder. Then, using your left hand, push up on right elbow and hold. Do the same with the left hand placed on the right shoulder. Repeat twice with each arm.

HAND, FINGER AND WRIST STRETCHES

First make a fist with both hands; then spread all fingers outward. Relax and repeat.

Especially important for computer and smartphone users!

DEEP BREATHING

Slowly inhale through your nose. Hold the breath for two seconds, then exhale through your mouth. Repeat.

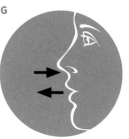

NECK TURNS

Holding your head upright, slowly turn it to one side and hold. Then slowly turn your head to the other side and hold. Next, slowly tip your head forward and hold.

Exercises without equipment

When travelling, you need to keep fit and flexible so you can enjoy the sights (and the food). Try these simple moves in your hotel room or on the beach.

① Child's pose Kneel and rest your hips on your heels. Touch head to floor and hold for up to 5 minutes.

② Shoulder stretch Lie on belly, and stretch arms out to side. Raise them just off the ground. Hold, then lower.

③ Cat stretch Inhale and raise chin and tailbone, so the spine curves downwards. Then exhale and arch the spine upwards. Repeat 10 times.

④ Hamstring strengthener Bend your knee back 90 degrees and hold for 5 seconds. Lower leg to the floor. Repeat 10 times, then change legs. (Good with weights attached to the ankles if you have them.)

⑤ Lunge Staying upright, step forward with one leg and hold. You'll feel a stretch in the front of your other leg.

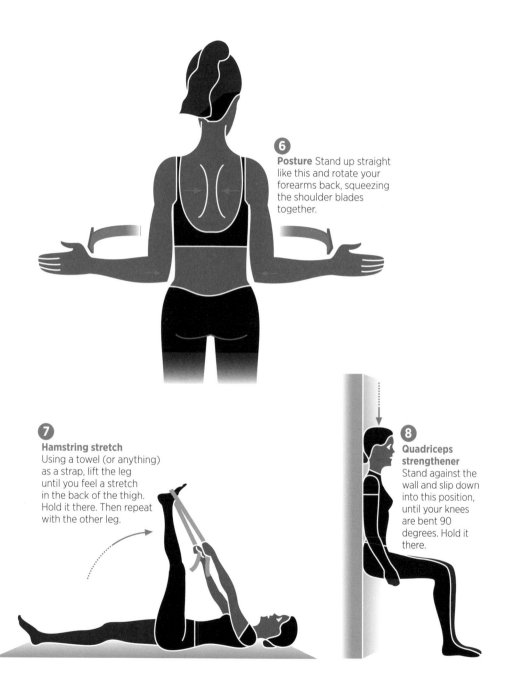

6
Posture Stand up straight like this and rotate your forearms back, squeezing the shoulder blades together.

7
Hamstring stretch
Using a towel (or anything) as a strap, lift the leg until you feel a stretch in the back of the thigh. Hold it there. Then repeat with the other leg.

8
Quadriceps strengthener
Stand against the wall and slip down into this position, until your knees are bent 90 degrees. Hold it there.

More moves without (real) exercise equipment

For instance, this could be a beach bucket with some sand in it, or a heavy book.

1
Lunging with some resistance

A Step forward with one leg. (Both knees should be bent.)

B

After swinging the bucket across your body, return it to the original position as you step forward with your other leg. Continue moving forward like this.

2
High kicks

Ⓐ

Ⓑ

(Hope you
don't need
this one!)

3

Shoulder and thigh stretches

Ⓐ Lie on belly with arms
and legs stretched out.

Ⓑ Raise opposite arms
and legs in a
continuous
flow.

Sun safety
Be a wise traveller; use these protective measures.

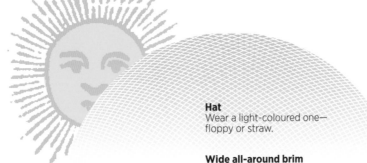

Hat
Wear a light-coloured one—
floppy or straw.

Wide all-around brim
Shading cheeks, ears and neck.

When you are driving
UV rays shine right through glass.
Apply an extra dollop of "drive-side"
protection to your arm, and the
side of your face closest to the
window, as well as both
hands on the driving wheel.

Sunglasses and eyes
Must have 100% UV protection.
Don't forget your eyelids. Find a
sunscreen that's opthalmologist
tested and fragrance free.

Lips
Since they have no melanin,
lips need special care. Buy a
waterproof sunscreen just for
them, clear enough to wear up
and over the lip line.

Perfume
It can cause a photo-
chemical reaction on skin.
Attracts bees, too.

Clothes
Protective covering *should*
include long-sleeved, tightly
woven, pale-coloured cover-ups,
that are loose fitting for comfort.

Medicine
Some prescriptions (topical
and nontopical) can cause
photosensitivity. Play safe.
Check with your pharmacist.

Exposure time = 1 hour

Sun exposure is cumulative. The rays you soak up, add up. Here are some typical exposure times for different activities. Make sure you have enough sunscreen, and that you use it liberally and often!

Watching a football game

Playing nine holes of golf

Window shopping

A day working in an office by the window

Eating lunch outdoors

Gardening

Jogging at noon

Skiing all day

Pushing a baby carriage, or a swing

Waterskiing

Walking the dog

Sun stuff

From SPF to UVA and UVB, what's a jargon-challenged traveller to do?

1 **What's in the Sun's rays?**

The parts of a sunbeam that most affect your skin are the **ultraviolet rays A and B,** and **infrared** rays.

These are the burning rays that turn your skin red, and may also affect its DNA.

These are the rays that can cause skin cancer.

These penetrate deep into the skin and damage its support structure. They inhibit the repair of UVB injury, cause changes in blood vessels and are responsible for premature skin ageing.

UVA
UVB
INFRARED

2 **The Sun's bounce-back effect**

3%
Grassy lawn, golf course

20%
Sand

45%
City concrete

3 What exactly is "SPF"?

It stands for Sun Protection Factor. The **number** (that follows "SPF") is a multiple of the amount of Sun time it would normally take your skin to start to burn **without protection.**

So, if you start to redden within **10 minutes** ...

you should apply a **SPF 15** sunscreen ...

and you'll be protected for **2.5 hours.**

10 minutes x 15 minutes = 150 minutes (2.5 hours)

Remember: **the higher the SPF, the greater the protection.**
SPF 15 is the lowest number recommended by most dermatologists.
SPF 30 is generally agreed to be the maximum required if you have a fair complexion, red hair or lots of freckles. (If you have all three, go up to SPF 50.)
Note: many sunscreens do not block UVA radiation. Use a broad-spectrum (UVA/UVB) sunscreen to address this.

4 Be careful in the Sun

Try to avoid the Sun completely during these hours:

10am–2pm

take a siesta instead!

(During daylight saving time, that's 11am–3pm.)

During these hours, avoid the Sun if you are ...

10am–3pm

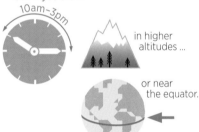

in higher altitudes ...

or near the equator.

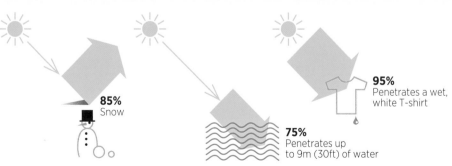

85% Snow

75% Penetrates up to 9m (30ft) of water

95% Penetrates a wet, white T-shirt

Dealing with snakebites

Most snakes kill their prey with constriction, but venomous snakes are found on every continent except Antarctica. Here's what to do, and not to do, if you or a fellow human are bitten.

Do this:

☑ **Wash** the bite with soap and water.

☑ Keep the affected body part **immobile,** and lower than the heart if possible.

☑ Call for medical help, or go to a **hospital** as quickly as you can.

☑ If you cannot get medical care within 30 minutes, wrap a crepe or elastic **bandage** 5-10cm (2-4in) above the bite to impede the flow of venom. But don't make it so tight as to cut off blood flow. (It should be loose enough to be able to slip a finger under it.)

☑ Take a **photo** of the snake if you can, or at least make some notes about its colour and size. This will help staff at the hospital identify it and administer the correct antivenin.

Don't do any of this:

☒ **Use ice** or hot packs.

☒ **Apply a tourniquet.**

☒ **Make incisions** of any kind to the wound.

☒ **Eat, drink or take medication.**

☒ **Apply mouth suction** to bite.
In addition, there's disagreement about the value of placing **suction cups** over the bite to draw out venom. Such devices are included in most commercially available snakebite kits, but many experts warn against using them.

☒ **Remove bandage** until in hospital.

☒ **Try to kill** the snake.

By the way, there's **no truth** in the idea that venomous snakes have slit, catlike pupils, while nonvenomous snakes have round pupils. Snakes have no eyelids, so to protect their eyes from bright lights (and when they are asleep), their pupils contract to a slit shape.

But, in the northeast USA (and only there),
here's a colour rule to follow:

If **RED** touches **BLACK**, you're OK, Jack.

If **RED** touches YELLOW, you're a dead fellow.

(king snake)

(coral snake—deadly)

All snakes have forked tongues. Since they have poor eyesight and no ears, the tongue is a snake's primary sense organ, relaying airborne scents to the mouth. This results in a mixture of taste and smell.

DEADLY DOZEN

Stay out of their way.
(Actually, leave ALL snakes alone.)

Hook-nosed sea snake
Coastlines of South Asia
Its venom is eight times more toxic than a cobra's.

Russell's viper
India

Inland taipan
Australia

Eastern brown
Australia

Black mamba
Africa
At 2.5m (8.2ft), it's one of the longest and fastest snakes. If a bite is not treated, the victim will probably die within 30 minutes.

Tiger rattlesnake
SW USA, NW Mexico

Boomslang
Africa

Blue krait
SE Asia, Indonesia
Its bite feels like a mosquito's, and it often strikes while the victim is asleep. They won't wake up ... ever.

Horned viper
Middle East, N. Africa

Tiger snake
Australia

Cobra
India
Medical upside: Alzheimer's researchers are looking at cobra venom as a possible therapy.

Puff adder
Africa

This list is based on *Snakes in Question*, by CH Ernst and GR Zug. Their 1996 paper ranked 80+ deadly snakes by the amount of their venom that's lethal to mice (called LD50). Snake venom works differently on different animals, including humans, but measuring the LD50 is the most common way to gauge a snake's venomosity.

Yoga on the road: the sun salutation

The sun salutation is a series of 12 poses performed in a single flow. It's often used as a warm-up routine before more vigorous poses. Even if you don't do any other yoga while you are travelling, do a couple of rounds of this; it's a good way to say hello to the day (even if there's no sun!).

First aid

You might not be a doctor, but you can help yourself, and others.

A little history

- There are records from the 11th century showing that religious knights provided care to pilgrims, and trained other knights to treat battlefield injuries.

- In 1863, four nations met in Geneva to form what has become the Red Cross. Initially the organisation's aim was to treat wounded soldiers on the battlefield.

- In the USA, the Civil War (1861–65) prompted Clara Barton to organise the American Red Cross.

- The term "first aid" was coined in England in 1878, at the same time that civilians were taught first aid.

- Today there are first aid training organisations in many countries including Australia, Canada, Ireland, Singapore and the Netherlands.

Simple principles

Preserve life
Prevent further harm
Promote recovery

All sounds good
to me. Let's go ...

Nosebleeds

1. Sit; lean forward slowly; keep the mouth open.

2. **Pinch the lower part of the nostrils; hold for 15 minutes.** (Victim breathes through the mouth.)

3. Release slowly. Don't touch the nose, or blow it; you might start the bleeding again.

4. If bleeding has not stopped after 20 minutes, seek medical attention.

Hiccups

Most of the time, hiccups are **not medically significant.** Doctors dismiss the many folk remedies. But if your favourite cure works, go with it!

1. The most efficient "cures" concentrate on relaxing or stimulating the diaphragm; many of them feature odd ways of drinking water.

2. So **try this one:** stand up; take a sip of water; turn your head upside down and swallow slowly.

Minor burns

1. Remove watches, bracelets, rings or constricting clothing before the burned area begins to swell.

2. **Hold the burn under cold running water** for a few minutes.

3. Apply a cold compress* until the pain diminishes.

4. Dress the area with clean (if possible, sterile) non-fluffy material.

Major burns

1. **If clothes are on fire, douse the victim with water.**

2. **Wrap the injured person in a blanket;** place him or her on the ground. Do not try to remove clothing that is stuck to wounds.

3. **Cover exposed burned areas** with clean, dry non-fluffy material to stop infection; secure with a bandage.

4. **DO NOT:**
   - use adhesive dressings
   - apply butter or oil
   - apply lotions or creams
   - prick burn blisters
   - use fluffy materials

Motion sickness

It's caused by constant movement of the organ of balance in the inner ear, and also by the anxiety produced by previous attacks.

1. Various drugs are available to prevent or control motion sickness. **Antihistamines** help if taken about an hour before the start of a journey.

2. **Tip:** tell sufferers to focus on a point on the horizon rather than on nearby objects.

Blisters

1. They are best left to heal by themselves.

2. **Do not prick or burst blisters,** because the underlying tissue could become infected.

   (The fluid inside a blister is a serum that has leaked from blood in the skin underneath after a minor injury, such as that caused by a tight-fitting shoe. The serum is sterile, and provides protection to the damaged tissue.)

Sunburn

1. Apply **calamine lotion** or sunburn cream.

2. Protect burned skin from further exposure.

3. Take analgesics (painkillers) to relieve tenderness.

4. Extreme burning may require a cream containing corticosteroid drugs prescribed by a doctor.

Heat stroke

Heat stroke differs from heat exhaustion (where the victim sweats profusely) in that sweating stops completely, the body becomes dry and flushed, and breathing is shallow.

1. **Seek medical help immediately.**

2. Move the victim to a cool shady place; remove clothing. Place the victim in a sitting position, leaning back slightly.

3. Cover with a wet sheet and keep it wet.

4. Fan with a magazine (or other suitable object) until their temperature drops to a normal range.

WHAT TO KEEP IN YOUR FIRST AID KIT

Just pack **necessities**—your kit must be portable.
- adhesive tape
- antiseptic cream
- antiseptic wipes
- aspirin
- bandages:
   absorbent gauze
   adhesive
   elastic
- calamine lotion
- foil or "space" blanket
- roll of sterile cotton
- rubbing alcohol
- safety pins
- scissors
- torch (check batteries!)
- tweezers

If possible, include a **mobile phone** (cellphone) in your kit. (Put an old one in there. It still needs a battery to turn it on, but even if your contract has expired, the emergency number for the country you are travelling in should still work.)

*A **cold compress** is a pad of material soaked in ice-cold water and held in place with a bandage. It reduces pain and swelling. (A compress that has been soaked in hot water increases the circulation and is useful for bringing boils to a head. A dry compress is used to stop bleeding from a wound.)

More **first aid**

Additional ways you can help in emergencies.

Diarrhoea

This is usually caused by food poisoning.

1 **To prevent dehydration,** dissolve 1 teaspoon of salt and 4 teaspoons of sugar in 9.5l (1qt) of water; drink 0.5l (1pt) of the mixture every hour.

2 Don't eat any solid food until the diarrhoea subsides.

3 If the condition persists for more than a week, or if there's blood visible, you should go to a doctor.

Removing a splinter

1 **Don't apply pressure or try squeezing to get it out.** (You might embed it further.)

2 Wash the area with soap and water. Pat dry; don't let the skin get soggy.

3 Inspect carefully: the angle the splinter entered will be its best route out!

There are several ways to remove splinters. Here are two interesting noninvasive methods.

Using baking soda:

1 Make a paste with a small amount of baking soda and water.

2 Put the mixture on a bandage and apply it to the affected area.

3 Leave it on for 24 hours, then remove.

4 The splinter should be sticking out of the skin, and should be easily removed with tweezers.

5 If necessary, repeat with new paste.

Using a potato:

1 Cut a potato into slices.

2 Place a slice on the affected area.

3 Hold it there, but don't apply pressure.

4 The potato should draw the splinter right out.

5 Optional celebration of successful splinter removal: put the rest of the potato on a skewer and cook it over the campfire.

Using a splint for a broken leg

Splints are used to prevent movement of a fractured limb. An improvised splint can be made from a piece of wood or a rolled-up magazine or newspaper.

1 If help is on the way, do not move the victim, but support the leg by putting one hand above the break, the other below it.

2 If the ambulance or other help is delayed, put a soft cloth around the splint then place it between the victim's knees and ankles.

3 Gently bring the uninjured leg toward the injured one.

4 Tie the ankles and feet together with a bandage in a figure-of-eight formation, secured on the uninjured side.

5 Tie bandages around the knees and thighs, avoiding the fracture site. All knots should be tied on the uninjured side.

6 Wait for help to arrive.

Sprained ankle

1 Make the victim as comfortable as possible.

2 **Apply a cold compress** (see "First Aid" spread) to the ankle; leave it on for 30 minutes.

3 Firmly bandage the lower leg and ankle (but not the toes) in a figure-of-eight formation.

4 Seek medical help. An x-ray may be needed.

Stings

1 Plants such as **nettles** carry tiny amounts of liquid that can irritate, but the effect wears off after an hour or so. Calamine lotion will soothe the irritation.

2 For a **jellyfish sting,** apply vinegar to inactivate the stinging liquid. Scrape off any fragments of tentacle; take an analgesic painkiller.

3 For a **scorpion bite,** take painkillers and apply a cold compress. (In some cases, antivenin may need to be given intravenously.)

Removing a fish hook

1 **If the hook is large or deeply embedded, go to a doctor at once.**

2 If it's a small hook, do not try to withdraw it the way it went in. Instead, **cut off the end of the hook** (including the circular loop that's attached to the fishing line), so that just a shaft of metal is left.

3 Swab the hook and surrounding area with rubbing alcohol.

4 Force the point of the hook forwards and up through the skin until it can be pulled out, making a **second puncture** in the skin.

5 Put some antibacterial cream and a bandage on the wounds.

There are other methods of removing fish hooks, but one way to avoid the problem altogether is to **use barbless hooks.** It's more fish-friendly if you are going to release the fish, and for you it's a painless way to get rid of a hook if you are caught by one.

Bleeding

1 Before tending to a victim's wound, **wash your hands** with soap and water if possible.

2 If a cut has dirt in it, rinse it under lukewarm water.

3 With a sterile gauze, dab the cut gently to dry it.

4 Cover with an adhesive bandage.

If it's a deep cut:

1 Raise the injured part and support it.

2 **Put a sterile dressing on the wound; apply firm pressure.**

3 If blood seeps through, don't remove the blood-soaked dressing (that might disturb clots and restart bleeding).

4 Put more dressings on top of the first one, and bandage them all together.

How to deliver a baby in an emergency

Remember this: most of the time, a baby delivers itself. Follow these pointers, though, and you'll make it easier for the mother.

If possible, have these things ready:

Two clean pieces of string, 22cm (9in) long, for tying the cord (shoelaces will do).

Sterilised scissors— boil them for 10 minutes and wrap them in a clean cloth.

Plastic bag for the afterbirth.

Soft blanket for the baby.

Container in case the mother vomits.

For some women, childbirth is a relatively painless experience. But others go through great pain. **Be prepared.**

1 **Wash your hands.**

2 You know the birth process is starting when muscles in the mother's uterus begin to contract at regular intervals. (If it's the mother's first baby, a good sign that the baby is nearly ready is when these **contractions are about 5 minutes apart and last from 40 to 90 seconds.)**

3 As the time between the contractions gets shorter, the mother feels them to be more intense. Her cervix dilates, and the mucus plug is discharged (her "water" breaks).

4 Contractions push the baby from the uterus to and through the vagina. As the baby emerges from the mother's body, **cradle the head but don't pull it.** The head usually comes out facing down, and returns to a normal position as the shoulders emerge (one at a time).

5 **Check if the umbilical cord is wrapped around the baby's neck.** If it is, slip it over the baby's head.

6 After the shoulders are out, the rest of the body should slide out easily with the next contraction.

7 **Wipe away any mucus** or blood from the baby's mouth.

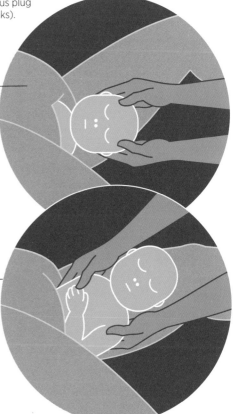

8 **Do not slap the baby on the back.** Instead, blow on the chest or tap the feet.

9 When the baby has been fully delivered,
tie the umbilical cord in two places.

10 **Cut the cord with
sterilised scissors.**
(The baby does
not feel this.)

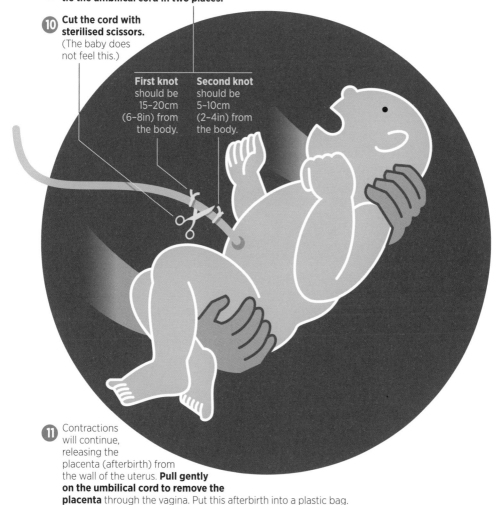

First knot
should be
15–20cm
(6–8in) from
the body.

Second knot
should be
5–10cm
(2–4in) from
the body.

11 Contractions
will continue,
releasing the
placenta (afterbirth) from
the wall of the uterus. **Pull gently
on the umbilical cord to remove the
placenta** through the vagina. Put this afterbirth into a plastic bag.

How to perform a tracheotomy

This is serious stuff. You'd only slice someone's throat after trying all other ways—including the Heimlich manoeuvre—to restore their ability to breathe.

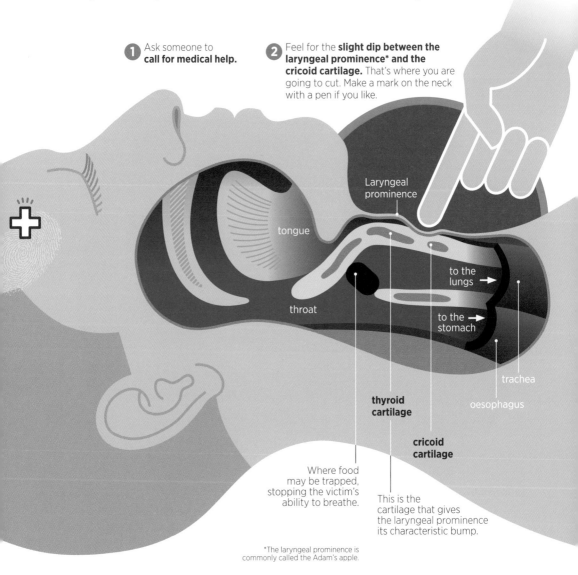

1 Ask someone to **call for medical help.**

2 Feel for the **slight dip between the laryngeal prominence* and the cricoid cartilage.** That's where you are going to cut. Make a mark on the neck with a pen if you like.

Laryngeal prominence

tongue

to the lungs

throat

to the stomach

trachea

oesophagus

thyroid cartilage

cricoid cartilage

Where food may be trapped, stopping the victim's ability to breathe.

This is the cartilage that gives the laryngeal prominence its characteristic bump.

*The laryngeal prominence is commonly called the Adam's apple.

3 With a clean, sharp razor, **make a horizontal cut** about 1cm (0.4in) across and 1cm (0.4in) deep. There should not be too much blood.

4 Open the cut slightly with your finger and **insert a straw into the cut.** (The straw should be the biggest you have. If you have only thin ones, use two. Substitutes could be the barrel of a pen or a rolled up card.)

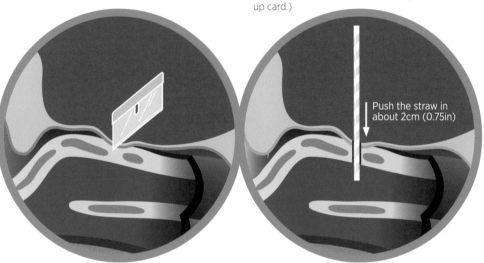

Push the straw in about 2cm (0.75in)

5 **Breathe into the straw quickly. Wait 5 seconds, then breathe again. Repeat once every 5 seconds.**

6 The whole process—from the failure of the Heimlich manoeuvre to the victim breathing on his or her own through the tube—must take **no longer than 3 minutes.** (3 minutes without oxygen means brain death.)

How to defend yourself

Arguing in Istanbul? Rowing in Tokyo? Here's hoping you don't end up having to defend yourself, but just in case, here are three ways to get out of a sticky situation. (Hint: wear all blue, he's the winner here).

Making your hotel room burglar proof

Some ways to stop yourself from being an easy target for thieves.

❶ BEFORE YOU GO ON A TRIP

- **Make a list** of your valuables, including models and serial numbers. You could take photos of them too. (Leave a copy of this at home too—you don't want your list to get stolen!)

- Consider **insuring** your valuables.

- In case you are robbed, it's a good idea to have **copies of all your important documents** (air tickets, passport, visas etc); keep one set in a separate spot to the originals, and give another copy to someone at home.

❷ WHEN YOU ARRIVE AT THE HOTEL

- When choosing your room, make sure the **entrance is well lit.** You may want to check if the hotel has security cameras. (Remember, travellers make great targets for thieves. You don't yet know your way around, or even who should be around.)

❸ WHENEVER YOU LEAVE YOUR ROOM

- **Leave the lights on.** You could leave the TV or the radio on too.

- **Close the blinds** so no one can see what's inside or if anyone is there.

- Don't forget to **lock the doors** and close the windows! (And the balcony door if you're lucky enough to have a balcony.)

- If you've got a **"Do not disturb"** sign then hang it on your door so that thieves will think the room is occupied.

- If there's a telephone in the room, **turn down the ringer** so that no one can hear it ring out.

- **Pack your belongings back into your suitcase** before you leave your room; lock it if you have a lock. If someone enters your room and there's nothing on display they may not bother to look for anything.

- **Don't return your key to the front desk** on leaving your hotel if the key and room number will be hanging behind the desk, visible to everyone. (And announcing that you're not in there!)

- Protect your valuables. **Don't leave any cash, jewellery or your passport in your room.** If you must, then make it hard for them to be found—don't leave them out in the open. Thieves will want to get in and out quickly.

- If the hotel has a **safe,** consider putting your valuables in it.

- If you need to leave your valuables, consider hiding them by using tape to **fasten them to the underside of a wardrobe** or another piece of furniture.

- **If you see anyone suspicious, let reception know.**

④ WHEN YOU ARE INSIDE YOUR ROOM

- Keep the door **locked** at all times when you're inside.

- If someone knocks on your door and you don't know who it is, **don't open it.**

- Place a **wedge under the door** or a chair under the handle or something against the door, so that if someone tries to open it while you're asleep you will know.

- You could even make **your own alarm system:** stack several glasses (or other objects that will make a noise) next to the door. If the door opens the objects will fall over and make enough noise to wake you. (Don't forget to test your system.)

- When you're sleeping, **separate your cash and credit cards/ATM cards** and put them in a few different locations.

⑤ IF YOU ARE BURGLED

- **Get out of your room;** the thief might still be in there!

- Call **hotel security** and the police.

Why must I turn off my mobile phone?

Read on; here's why!

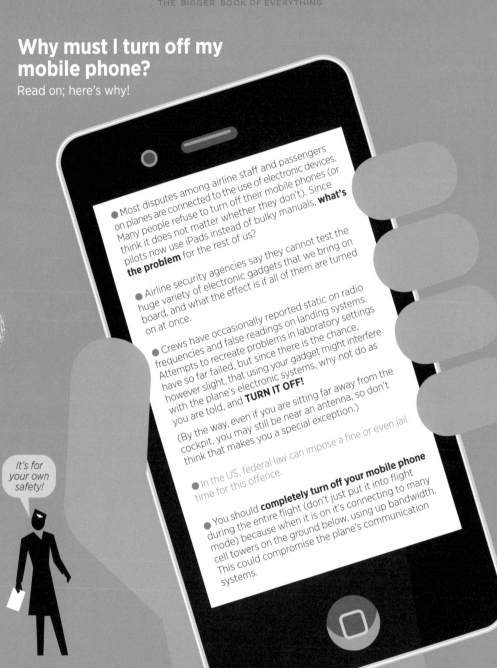

- Most disputes among airline staff and passengers on planes are connected to the use of electronic devices. Many people refuse to turn off their mobile phones (or think it does not matter whether they don't). Since pilots now use iPads instead of bulky manuals, **what's the problem** for the rest of us?

- Airline security agencies say they cannot test the huge variety of electronic gadgets that we bring on board, and what the effect is if all of them are turned on at once.

- Crews have occasionally reported static on radio frequencies and false readings on landing systems. Attempts to recreate problems in laboratory settings have so far failed, but since there is the chance, however slight, that using your gadget might interfere with the plane's electronic systems, why not do as you are told, and **TURN IT OFF!**

  (By the way, even if you are sitting far away from the cockpit, you may still be near an antenna, so don't think that makes you a special exception.)

- In the US, federal law can impose a fine or even jail time for this offence.

- You should **completely turn off your mobile phone** during the entire flight (don't just put it into flight mode) because when it is on it's connecting to many cell towers on the ground below, using up bandwidth. This could compromise the plane's communication systems.

It's for your own safety!

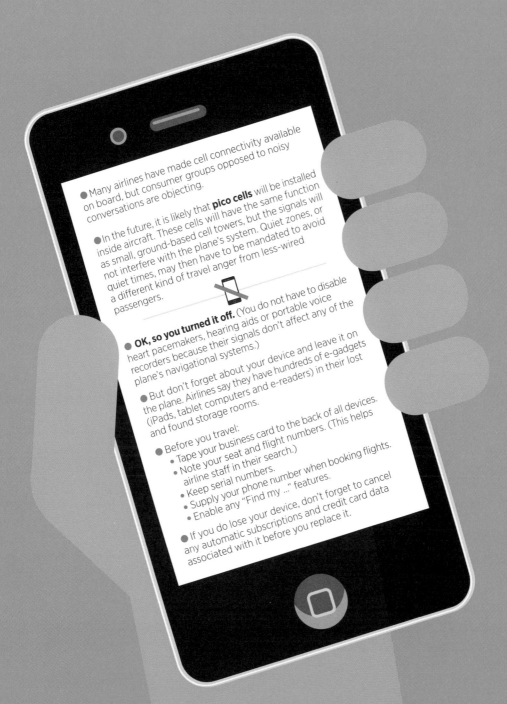

- Many airlines have made cell connectivity available on board, but consumer groups opposed to noisy conversations are objecting.

- In the future, it is likely that **pico cells** will be installed inside aircraft. These cells will have the same function as small, ground-based cell towers, but the signals will not interfere with the plane's system. Quiet zones, or quiet times, may then have to be mandated to avoid a different kind of travel anger from less-wired passengers.

- **OK, so you turned it off.** (You do not have to disable heart pacemakers, hearing aids or portable voice recorders because their signals don't affect any of the plane's navigational systems.)

- But don't forget about your device and leave it on the plane. Airlines say they have hundreds of e-gadgets (iPads, tablet computers and e-readers) in their lost and found storage rooms.

- Before you travel:
  - Tape your business card to the back of all devices.
  - Note your seat and flight numbers. (This helps airline staff in their search.)
  - Keep serial numbers.
  - Supply your phone number when booking flights.
  - Enable any "Find my ..." features.

- If you do lose your device, don't forget to cancel any automatic subscriptions and credit card data associated with it before you replace it.

How to avoid being hit by lightning

Don't want to get fried? Read on.

1 When you hear thunder, you can be pretty sure that lightning will follow.

2 If the time between a flash of lightning and the sound of thunder is less than 30 seconds (and you are outdoors), **move to a safe place.**

3 If you are anywhere above the treeline or in an open field, **MOVE!**

4 But if there's nowhere to go, **kneel with your hands on the ground.** Bow your head forward.

5 **DON'T stand near or go into any of these places:**

Safe places to go

● **Large enclosed buildings.** Once inside, avoid contact with showers, sinks, metal doors and window frames, as well as electrical outlets and cords, telephones and televisions—in fact anything that's wired.

● **Fully enclosed cars, trucks, buses and vans.** When you are inside, avoid contact with metal surfaces in these vehicles.

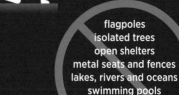

flagpoles
isolated trees
open shelters
metal seats and fences
lakes, rivers and oceans
swimming pools
convertibles
golf carts

What *is* lightning, anyway?

● Scientists are still debating the details of how lightning occurs, but it's an atmospheric electrical discharge—a spark—usually associated with cumulonimbus clouds.

Lightning can travel at speeds up to 220,000km/h (140,000mph) and can reach
● a temperature of 30,000°C (54,000°F).

There are 16 million lightning storms in the world each year.
●

About 70% of lightning occurs in the tropics (where most thunderstorms happen).
●

The most afflicted spot is the village of Kifuka, elevation 975m (3200ft), in the Democratic
● Republic of the Congo. It receives an amazing 158 lightning strikes per square kilometre (0.39 square miles) a year.

6 While storms usually occur when it's dark (or at least cloudy), the danger from lightning can exist in sunshine, when the sky is clear.

How to drive in the snow

①　PREPARE!

❄ **Keep these items somewhere in the car:**
flashlight • jumper cables • nylon tow strap • energy bars • drinking water • shovel • ice scraper • warm blanket • book or magazine to keep you occupied until help comes.

❄ **Brush away all snow.** When it blows off it might obstruct your view. The weight of snow on the roof of a car increases the car's stopping distance and alters its centre of gravity.

❄ **Clear ice and snow from the base of the windscreen.** Wipers won't clog as quickly, and the vent there is often the fresh-air intake.

❄ **Keep fuel tank at least half full.** This keeps weight over the rear wheels. It also prevents condensation from forming in the tank and causing gas-line freezing.

❄ **Keep all headlights and rear lights clean.** You'll see and be seen.

③　IF YOU GET STUCK

❄ **Don't spin the wheels.** Friction causes heat. A puddle of water will form under the wheels and turn to ice.

❄ **Dig snow out from under the car.** This will allow the wheels to rest firmly on the ground and gain traction.

❄ **If stranded, stay in the car.** It provides shelter and will be visible to rescuers. It's safe to run the engine for heat as long as you **keep the tailpipe area clear of snow.**

❄ **Put floor mats down for traction.**

② DRIVE (carefully!)

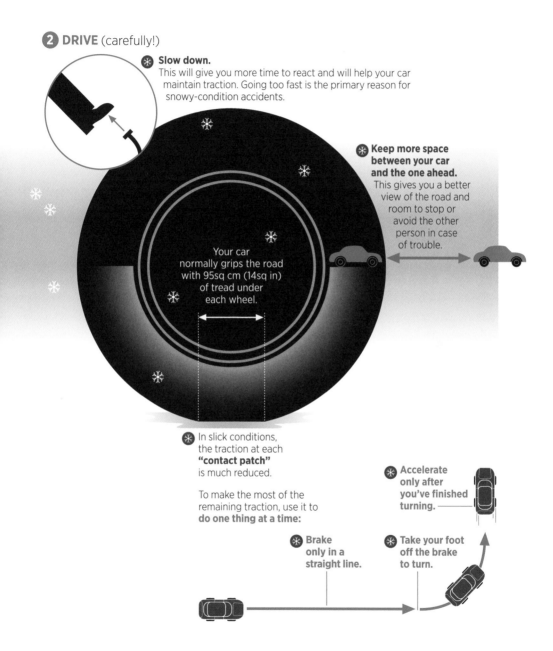

Slow down.
This will give you more time to react and will help your car maintain traction. Going too fast is the primary reason for snowy-condition accidents.

Keep more space between your car and the one ahead.
This gives you a better view of the road and room to stop or avoid the other person in case of trouble.

Your car normally grips the road with 95sq cm (14sq in) of tread under each wheel.

In slick conditions, the traction at each **"contact patch"** is much reduced.

To make the most of the remaining traction, use it to **do one thing at a time:**

Accelerate only after you've finished turning.

Brake only in a straight line.

Take your foot off the brake to turn.

How to be a lifeguard

Are you are already a sun and sand addict? How about being part beach police officer and part paramedic?

Yes? Well, you must:

1 be a strong swimmer!

2 be trained in first aid and lifesaving techniques, including CPR.

3 able to confidently enforce beach rules.

4 concentrate for long periods (when nothing seems to be happening).

5 anticipate potential problems.

6 act quickly in an emergency.

And you'll need a

- whistle
- flotation device
- high lookout seat
- 3m (10ft) rescue board

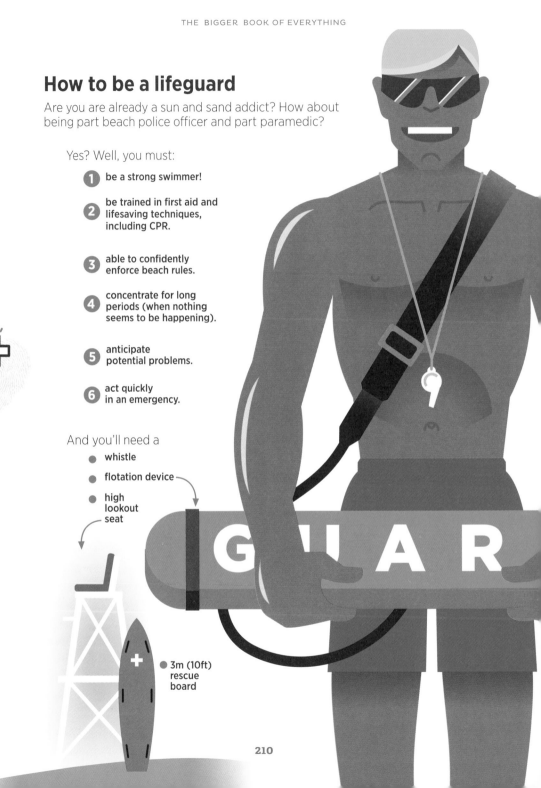

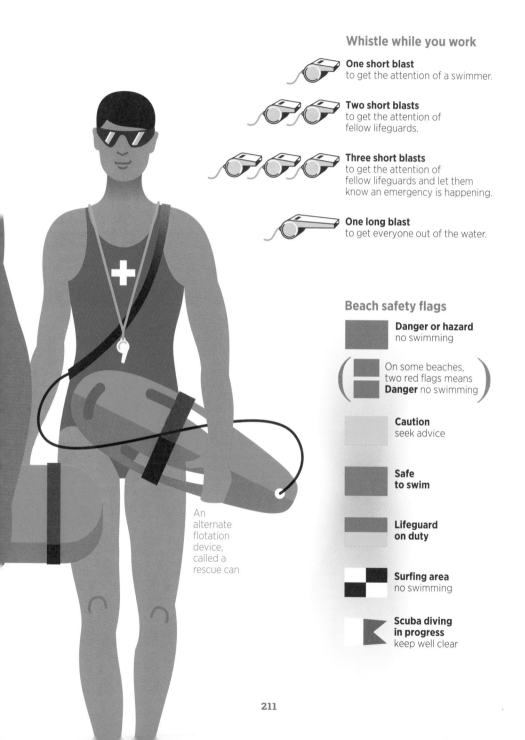

Whistle while you work

One short blast
to get the attention of a swimmer.

Two short blasts
to get the attention of
fellow lifeguards.

Three short blasts
to get the attention of
fellow lifeguards and let them
know an emergency is happening.

One long blast
to get everyone out of the water.

Beach safety flags

Danger or hazard
no swimming

On some beaches,
two red flags means
Danger no swimming

Caution
seek advice

Safe
to swim

Lifeguard
on duty

Surfing area
no swimming

Scuba diving
in progress
keep well clear

An
alternate
flotation
device,
called a
rescue can

Aaaaah! that feels good!

After a long hike, let a masseur, or masseuse, apply pressure to your muscles and connective tissue, using hands and fingers (and less often, their elbows, knees or forearms).

What can a massage do?
- relieve muscle pain
- relieve mental anxiety
- reduce blood pressure and heart rate
- restore energy
- provide feelings of calm and relaxation

Naked? Only if you feel comfortable with that.

Oils
All sorts are used, including:

Your face rests comfortably in a horseshoe-shaped padded ring.

- almond
- coconut
- grape seed
- jojoba
- olive
- pecan
- macadamia
- sesame
- baby oil

Enjoy the soft music

or a mixture!

What makes a good masseur?

- Friendly table-side manner
- A thorough knowledge of anatomy and physiology
- Strong hands (and a strong physique: it's exhausting work)
- Good intuitition and the confidence to know how to help the client
- Having a fast laundry service!

Different types
These are the most popular:

- accupressure — a traditional Chinese method; pressure is applied to acupuncture points
- craniosacral — light touches to the skull, face, spine and pelvis relieve tension
- hot stone massage — smooth, water-heated rocks apply pressure and heat
- reflexology — massaging hands and feet; reflexes there relate to every system in the body
- reiki* — hand and palm strokes are used to relieve ailments
- shiatsu* — finger and palm pressure
- Swedish — the classic treatment; long flowing strokes
- Thai massage — deep full-body massage applied from the feet up

*While popular, these are not shown to have much medical benefit.

The padded table top is lined with a clean sheet.

Mobile masseurs use folding tables to treat people in their homes or offices. (Be sympathetic when they come; the tables are not that light!)

Nasty, wiggly things

Parasites are scary to look at and do scary things to us.
Parasitologists develop drugs to treat the diseases they cause.

**Humans are hosts to 300 species of parasitic worms
and 70 species of protozoa that are invisible to our eyes.**
Being a host means that these organisms can live
on or inside us.*

Plasmodium

How does it get into you?
Mosquito bites

What does it cause? Malaria

Where is it prevalent? 87 countries,
including sub-Saharan Africa, India,
China, Brazil and most of SE Asia.
An estimated 435,000 people died
of malaria in 2017.

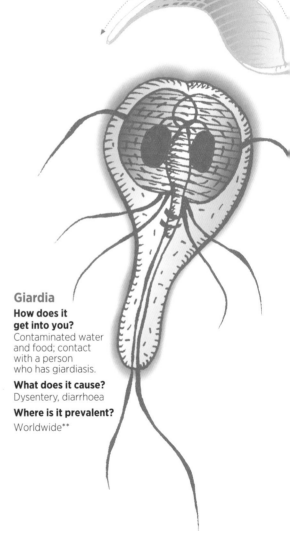

Giardia

**How does it
get into you?**
Contaminated water
and food; contact
with a person
who has giardiasis.

What does it cause?
Dysentery, diarrhoea

Where is it prevalent?
Worldwide**

*Endoparasites live inside
us; ectoparasites live
"outside"—but just under
the skin, like the tick on
the next page.

** Every continent
except Antarctica

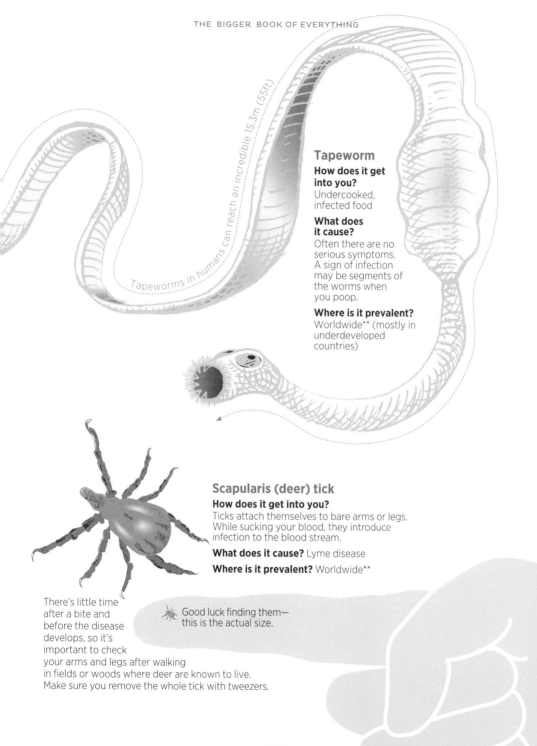

Tapeworms in humans can reach an incredible 15.3m (55ft)

Tapeworm

How does it get into you?
Undercooked, infected food

What does it cause?
Often there are no serious symptoms. A sign of infection may be segments of the worms when you poop.

Where is it prevalent?
Worldwide** (mostly in underdeveloped countries)

Scapularis (deer) tick

How does it get into you?
Ticks attach themselves to bare arms or legs. While sucking your blood, they introduce infection to the blood stream.

What does it cause? Lyme disease

Where is it prevalent? Worldwide**

There's little time after a bite and before the disease develops, so it's important to check your arms and legs after walking in fields or woods where deer are known to live. Make sure you remove the whole tick with tweezers.

Good luck finding them—this is the actual size.

What a naturopath does

Naturopathy is the treatment of illness by studying underlying causes rather than symptoms. The naturopathic doctor teaches patients to be responsible for their own health—it's easier to prevent a disease than to treat one.

● Advocating a healthy attitude, lifestyle and diet are part of the treatment, as are certain natural extracts.

● **Here are some of the most popular botanicals.**
(And where you can gather them)

Cranberry
for urinary tract
problems
(North America)

Garlic
to lower
cholesterol
(widely available)

St. John's Wort
for menopause
(widely available)

Black Cohosh
for menopause
(North America)

Soy
for menopause
(North America, Brazil,
Argentina, China, India)

Note: many studies have been done on the
effectiveness of these supplements and naturopathic medicine
as a whole. Not all of them have been complimentary.

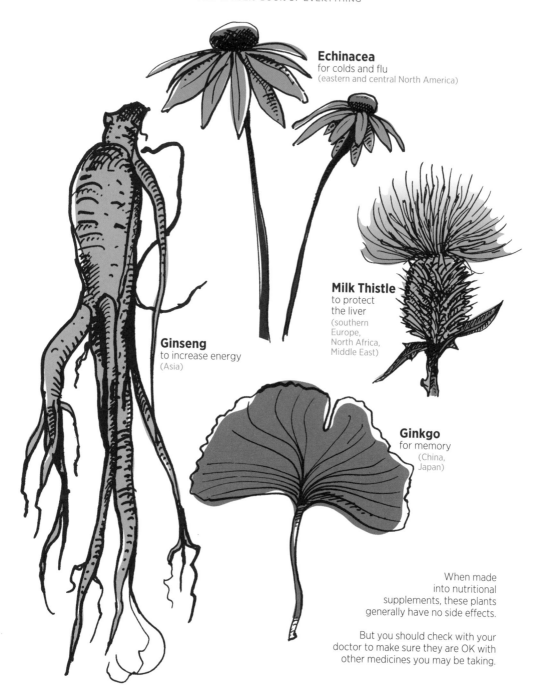

Echinacea
for colds and flu
(eastern and central North America)

Milk Thistle
to protect
the liver
(southern
Europe,
North Africa,
Middle East)

Ginseng
to increase energy
(Asia)

Ginkgo
for memory
(China,
Japan)

When made
into nutritional
supplements, these plants
generally have no side effects.

But you should check with your
doctor to make sure they are OK with
other medicines you may be taking.

Staying in shape

You don't need expensive machines to keep fit.
Here are six basic exercises to learn.
The **green ones are the easiest, blue a bit harder, red the most painful!**

To increase range of motion

1 Kneel on left knee; both hands on the mat.
Stretch right leg out; raise right arm to
the 12 o'clock position.
Slowly lower the arm,
then raise again.

Repeat 5 times.

Repeat on the
other side.

As you rotate, keep your hand facing forward.

Open your chest.

2 Start in the push-up
position. Lift one
arm to 12 o'clock.
Slowly lower the
arm, then
raise again.

Repeat 5 times.

Repeat on the
other side.

3 Start in the push up position, gripping weights.
Lift weight with a straight arm to 12 o'clock.
Slowly lower the arm, then raise again.

Repeat 5 times.

Repeat on the other side.

Keep your stomach drawn in.

Start with 2.5kg (5lbs) weights

To strengthen torso and hips

4 Lie on your back with knees bent and hands on hips. Push hips up, tilting them backwards as you lift yourself up to the horizontal position.

Repeat 10 times.

Visualise pouring water out towards the back.

5 Place yourself on the ball. Lower hips slowly (a), tilt pelvis, then lift up (b).

Repeat 10 times.

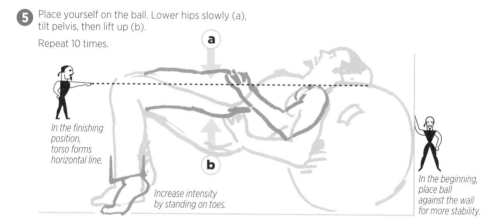

a

b

In the finishing position, torso forms horizontal line.

Increase intensity by standing on toes.

In the beginning, place ball against the wall for more stability.

6 Same position as before, but use weights for extra resistance.

Start with 4.5kg (10lbs)

Exercise balls are slightly squishy, inflated rubber spheres. They come in various sizes.

Ouch! Do-it-yourself dentistry

Your teeth are pretty strong, but accidents happen.
Here's how to alleviate some of the pain (and possible infection)
when you break a tooth. But you should see a real dentist quickly!

1 There are three different levels of damage:

● **chip** } more   When a large piece of tooth breaks ➡ Exposure to saliva, air or hold or
● **break** } serious   off, the nerve may be exposed.   cold food can cause real pain.

● **fracture** You might not notice a
minor crack at first.
But later, you may feel
pain if the damage
extends to the nerve, or
when you put pressure
on the tooth when
chewing food.

— enamel
— dentin
— pulp
— nerves

2 **Keep the broken
piece if you can.**
Pay attention
when you are
eating nuts:
they are a big
culprit! Don't
swallow if you
sense a problem;
spit it all out.
(Apologise if
you are with
others.)

3rd molar
(wisdom)

2nd molar

1st molar

premolar

premolar

canine

incisor

incisc

**IN THE
MOUTH** ↗
What you can
do for yourself
or others

BELOW
What a dentist ↓
can do for you

🦷 **Filling** is for small breaks.

🦷 **Bonding** fits a resin copy of the
tooth over the broken piece.

🦷 **Crowns or caps** are used for bigger breaks. The
dentist files the broken tooth down and "caps"
it with a model of the whole tooth.

🦷 **Veneers**—porcelain or resin slip covers—are usually fitted to front teeth.

🦷 **Root canals** are needed when the pulp of the tooth is damaged and opened
up to possible infection. After cleaning, the tooth is capped. This one hurts!

3 Take a painkiller if necessary.

An over-the-counter non-steroidal anti-inflammatory drug (NSAID) such as ibuprofen, or a pain medicine such as acetaminophen will help until a dentist prescribes something stronger.

6 Cover jagged or sharp tooth edges with paraffin wax.

If you don't have any paraffin wax (I know I don't!) use sugarless chewing gum instead. If you can't reach a dentist but can get to a chemist, buy temporary dental cement, and cover the tooth with that.

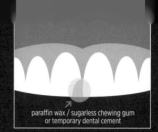

paraffin wax / sugarless chewing gum or temporary dental cement

4 Rinse your mouth, then gargle with salt water.

This'll help stop possible infection.

7 Use a cold compress to reduce swelling and pain.

This will make you more comfortable if you have to wait for treatment.

(A cold compress is a pad of material soaked in ice-cold water and held in place with a bandage, or just your hand.)

If you must, take another painkiller, but never exceed the recommended dosage.

5 To stop bleeding, hold a pad of gauze (or bunched up tissue) to the broken tooth for 10 minutes.

If this doesn't work, rinse your mouth with cold water. (The cold will contract blood vessels.)

← same as the other side! →

REMEMBER
You should **see a dentist** whenever you feel sensitivity in your mouth, especially when you are eating or from changes in temperature. Pain is an indication that a break or fracture may have damaged the nerve or the pulp (see cross-section above) in your tooth.

OTHER FUN STUFF

Roadtrip! Let's go to weirdly named places!

Americans give their towns, cities and unincorporated communities the oddest, sexiest, silliest names. Some of them are slightly naughty, too, so if you're offended by that sort of thing, please turn the page.

OK, the rest of you, have a nice trip!

&!

Washington
• Stuck

• Humptulips

Boring   Oregon
• Zigzag
• Riddle

California   Nevada
Likely   Welcome •

Bliss   You
Bet
Rough &
Ready
• Bummerville

Montana
Ynot •

Lame Deer
•

Idaho
Wyoming
Dickshooter •   Ten Sleep •
• Riddle

Hardup
•
He Flys
•

N. Dakota   Ops
• Zap
Flasher
•

S. Dakota
• Jolly Dump
Igloo
• Oral

Nebraska

Jay Em •

Colorado
Hygiene
•
Parachute
•

Surpri
Funk •

Kansas
Radiun

Utah
Arizona
Chloride
•
• Bagdad
Zzyzx   Humbug
•

New Mexico
Truth or
Consequences
•

Oklahoma

Texas
Happy
•
Heckvill •

Earth

• Why
Wink

Where to next? Toad Suck, Arkansas?

All names guaranteed real. (You can't make this stuff up.)

Minnesota
Embarrass
Luck
Iamalone
Michigan
Moon
Knockemstiff
Maine
• Purgatory
Vermont
Notown •
New York
Climax •
Massachusetts
Looneyville •
Iowa
Wisconsin
Hell
Pennsylvania
Economy
Effort •
New Jersey
Illinois
Indiana
Ohio
Intercourse •
• Dicktown
What
Cheer
South
Pole
• Dull
on
Love
French
Lick
Virginia
Missouri
• Conception
Speed •
W. Virginia
Normal
• New
• Fanny
Erection
Tightwad
s
• Peculiar
Kentucky
Tennessee
N. Carolina
• Horneytown
oss
Yum Yum
Erect •
ay
Arkansas
• Yell
S. Carolina
Tick Bite
Toad Suck
Alabama Georgia
nce
Turkey
Scratch
Mississippi
• Ninety Six
Eclectic
• Ideal
Cash
Hooker
Whynot
Enigma
Hopeulikeit
Ding
Hole
Dong
Louisiana
Two
Florida
Cut &
• Cut Off
Egg
• Doctor
Shoot
Phillips
st

Not to be outdone in the world of odd names, a villager from **Dull**, in the Scottish county of Perthshire, has proposed that **Boring** in Oregon be named sister town to Dull. (Just wondering ... why wasn't Dull, Ohio, chosen?)

By the way, it's thought that the word "dull" meant "meadow" in Gaelic.

Scotland
• Dull

(And just for the record, Boring, Oregon, is named after its founder, William H Boring.)

Wales
England

Map drawn to the same scale as the United States.

Space stuff 1: how to greet an alien

Essential etiquette and survival tips for when that unexpected visitor to Earth arrives.
(Some things on this page are from the fictional side of science.)

1 If you have time, quickly change into something green. All aliens are green. (You know that.)

2 With your two eyes, look him/her/himmer in the eye.

3 Wave arms—in the welcome position, not the *yikes!* position. *Easily confused*

4 Offer a drink. (Oh wait, they don't have hands—forget this.)

5 Start a conversation. (You have to know the language for this step. Could be awkward.)

BUT *(and it's a big, hairy but ...)*

if he/she/heshe looks aggressive ...

6 Run away.

&!

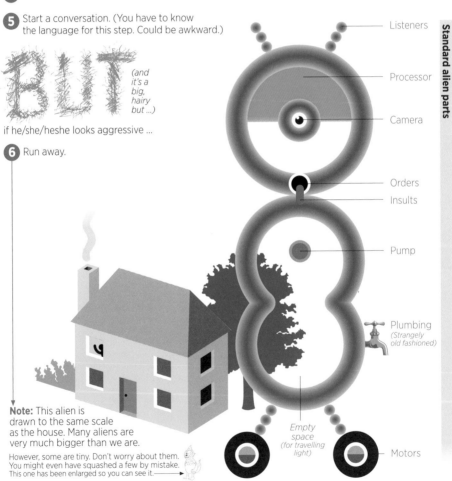

Standard alien parts

- Listeners
- Processor
- Camera
- Orders
- Insults
- Pump
- Plumbing *(Strangely old fashioned)*
- *Empty space (for travelling light)*
- Motors

Note: This alien is drawn to the same scale as the house. Many aliens are very much bigger than we are.

However, some are tiny. Don't worry about them. You might even have squashed a few by mistake. This one has been enlarged so you can see it.

Space stuff 2: real tourism

Going to the moon? Don't laugh, commercial space flights are coming—eventually.

The estimated price is $250,000 for a flight on Richard Branson's Virgin Galactic *VSS Unity*, starting in 2020. (Virgin's *SpaceShipTwo* suffered a fatal crash in 2014.)

Jeff Bezos will soon be offering flights aboard his *Blue Origin.* (The third major player in this domestic space race, Elon Musk's Space X vehicle *Crew Dragon,* is contracted to shuttle astronauts to the international space station. Musk's company is a long way behind schedule, and the *Crew Dragon* capsule was destroyed in an explosion in 2019.)

Branson and Bezos plan to take tourists just 62 miles up into space, where they will be weightless for about five minutes. These first trips will be short—about 30 minutes. When space tourism is ready to take you to or around the moon (Branson thinks that won't be until 2043), it'll take about 9 hours. Jupiter? About 13 months.

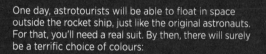

One day, astrotourists will be able to float in space outside the rocket ship, just like the original astronauts. For that, you'll need a real suit. By then, there will surely be a terrific choice of colours:

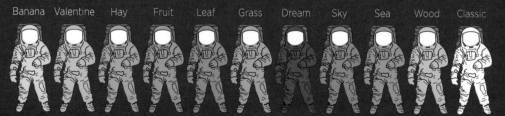

Banana   Valentine   Hay   Fruit   Leaf   Grass   Dream   Sky   Sea   Wood   Classic

An emergency joke kit

Perhaps your flight has been cancelled and you are stuck at the airport for hours waiting for seats on another plane. You'll need a sense of humour. Try this.

There must be a joke in here somewhere!

I don't see one.

① The characters
Pick three from this list

a plumber

a weightlifter

a lawyer

a scholar

a monkey

an ant

a grasshopper

an elephant

a magician

a psychiatrist

an alien

Miss Universe

God

② Their destination
Pick one

walk into ...

a bar

a bullfight

a gymnasium

a birthday party

a toyshop

a rock concert

a funeral parlour

a wedding

a kitchen

a museum

a muddy river

an ice-fishing hut

a xebec*

*Look it up!

3

4

5

What they say *(feel free to change the order of these in any way you like)*

the
[first character you picked]
says ...

hello

who's here?

I'm hungry

happy birthday!

knock, knock

it's hot in here

12 porcupines sat
down in a circle

my father was blind

on Tuesday it'll
be exactly 20 years

how do you feel?

I've got sand in my toes

why are we here?

the
[next character]
says ...

who's there?

I'm thirsty

I can't see anyone

that's stupid

I don't know

nice legs

I'm a vegetarian

it's just too big

I'm cold

so what?

my antennae

Van Gogh

what's to eat?

the
[last character]
says ...

it's only 4pm

that'll be €100

it's a small world

eight times a day

I'll have another

he's dead

just add water

I Googled it

my dog ate it

NUTS!

that joke is older
than I am

whatever

#!*@&!?

How to play croquet

Six hundred years ago, in France, shepherds played *"paille-maille"*, a stick-and-ball game. *Paille-maille* (meaning "ball and mallet") became "pall-mall" when it arrived in England 200 years later during the reign of Charles II. Apparently the king was a fan.

Alternate roots
There's another story about the game's origin, which claims that it came to England from Ireland in 1850, where it was called "cookey". In England it became an organised sport, called "croquet", in 1868.

Anyone for tennis?
Croquet's heyday was short-lived. By the 1870s tennis was more popular, with the club at Wimbledon converting some of its croquet lawns into tennis courts. (It's still officially called the All England Lawn Tennis and Croquet Club.) It was an Olympic sport in 1900, but never again. However in 2005, scientists played croquet at the South Pole.

Croquet balls are made of ceramic, wood or cork-filled plastic.
◄————This is the actual size.————►
Croquet can be played by two people or two teams of two. (Part of the game's attraction in the 1860s was that both men and women could play.)

If four people are playing, one team takes the blue and black balls, the other the red and yellow.

If two people are playing, one person takes both the blue and black balls, the other the red and yellow.

The order of play is blue, red, black, yellow.

The ball weighs about 0.5kg (16oz).

Anyone for croquet?
Today there are some 170 clubs in England and Wales associated with the Croquet Association, and in the USA (where the hoops are called wickets*) there are roughly 200 croquet clubs, plus more attached to universities and colleges.

Variations
Extreme Croquet was thought up in the USA in 1920. It's played in the wild, over difficult terrain—in woods or lowland marshes—with heavy duty equipment. The first known extreme club was started in Sweden in 1975.
Gateball was invented in Japan in 1947. Today it's played there and in other parts of east and southeast Asia, and the Americas. It's fast and competitive.
Bicycle Croquet is played on bicycles. Duh.

*Did someone get cricket and croquet mixed up in America? The names of the games might sound a bit alike, but that's no excuse. A hoop is a hoop (balls go through them), but cricket's wicket is a very different thing. For a start, it consists of three wooden sticks (called stumps) with separate wooden "bails" balanced on top ...

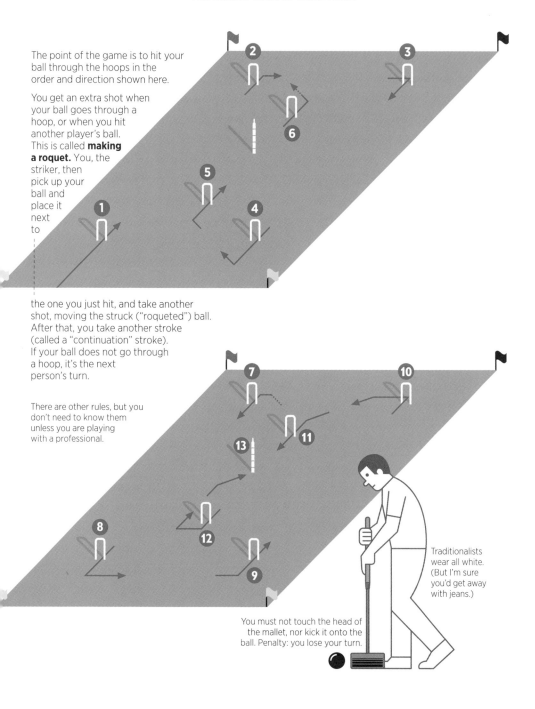

The point of the game is to hit your ball through the hoops in the order and direction shown here.

You get an extra shot when your ball goes through a hoop, or when you hit another player's ball. This is called **making a roquet.** You, the striker, then pick up your ball and place it next to the one you just hit, and take another shot, moving the struck ("roqueted") ball. After that, you take another stroke (called a "continuation" stroke). If your ball does not go through a hoop, it's the next person's turn.

There are other rules, but you don't need to know them unless you are playing with a professional.

Traditionalists wear all white. (But I'm sure you'd get away with jeans.)

You must not touch the head of the mallet, nor kick it onto the ball. Penalty: you lose your turn.

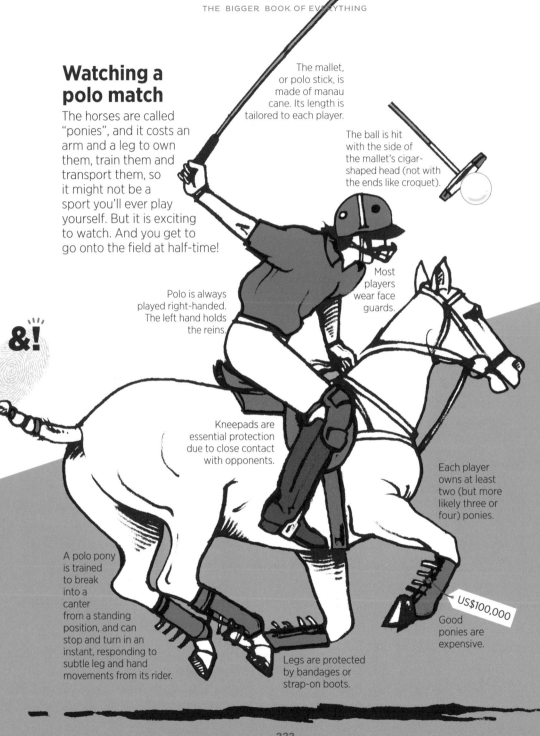

Watching a polo match

The horses are called "ponies", and it costs an arm and a leg to own them, train them and transport them, so it might not be a sport you'll ever play yourself. But it is exciting to watch. And you get to go onto the field at half-time!

The mallet, or polo stick, is made of manau cane. Its length is tailored to each player.

The ball is hit with the side of the mallet's cigar-shaped head (not with the ends like croquet).

Polo is always played right-handed. The left hand holds the reins.

Most players wear face guards.

Kneepads are essential protection due to close contact with opponents.

Each player owns at least two (but more likely three or four) ponies.

A polo pony is trained to break into a canter from a standing position, and can stop and turn in an instant, responding to subtle leg and hand movements from its rider.

&!

US$100,000

Good ponies are expensive.

Legs are protected by bandages or strap-on boots.

Rules

 The simple point of the game is to hit the ball through the opponents' goalposts.

 Usually there are six 7-minute **"chukkas"**.

 There's a 4-minute rest between each chukka. Players must change their horses. No horse can play more than two chukkas in a game.

④ At half-time, there's a 10-minute break, when spectators are invited onto the field for the tradition of **"divot stomping"** (replacing the turf the horses have messed up).

 The most important rule is **the right of way, or line of the running ball.** This is the route that a ball takes as it rolls forward along the ground. The player who hits the ball (the black icon below) has this "right of way".

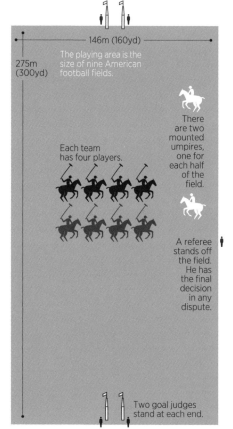

146m (160yd)

275m (300yd)

The playing area is the size of nine American football fields.

Each team has four players.

There are two mounted umpires, one for each half of the field.

A referee stands off the field. He has the final decision in any dispute.

Two goal judges stand at each end.

 If an opponent (blue icon) can reach the ball without getting in the way of the hitter, he* assumes the right of way.

*Or "she". Polo is one of those sports where men and women compete equally.

A ^{very!} brief history

● The modern game originated in **India** in the 1830s.

● British settlers took polo to **Argentina** in 1875, where it was enthusiastically embraced. By 1924, the official Argentine team was good enough to win the gold medal at the Paris Olympics.

● Today, the most important world-class polo tournaments are held in Argentina, but it's played in about 80 other countries.

Variations

● **Snow polo** is played on compacted snow or a frozen lake.

● Nonequine variants include: **bicycle, camel, canoe, elephant, golf cart, Segway and yak.**

● In East Africa, **moto-polo** is very popular. One person drives at speeds of 70km/h (44mph), while another sits behind holding a short mallet. One important rule: no sticking the mallet into an opponent's wheels.

Let's go by *fast* train

The world speed record of 574.8km/h (357.2mph) for a conventionally wheeled train was set by the French TGV (Train à Grande Vitesse) in 2007. First proposed in France in the 1960s, the TGV's first run, from Paris to Lyon, was in 1981.

In 1964, Japan's Bullet Train (Shinkansen) became the first high-speed train. This was followed by the Russian ER200 (also in 1964), and Britain's Intercity 125 in 1976. Belgium, Italy, Spain and Germany have built their own high-speed networks, linking with France's lines.

WHAT MAKES THE TGV SO SPEEDY?

The train was originally going to be powered by gas turbines, but after the gas crisis of 1973, plans changed to electricity carried in overhead cables and supplied by France's new nuclear power plants.

● **Connecting the pieces**
The wheels are attached to bogies that straddle two cars. This halves the number of wheels needed, saving weight. The cars are semipermanently attached to each other, making the whole "trainset" more rigid and improving aerodynamics.

● **High-speed power source**
Overhead electrical wires allow the trains themselves to be lighter.

● **Few ups and downs**
No incline on the track is more than 3.5%.

● **Gentler curves in the track**
A 5km (3 mile) turning radius is considered tight.

● **Light body**
It's made from aircraft-grade aluminium. This minimises the overall weight of the train.

Oo la la! Eet goes very fast!

Oui, and zey eet us on board!

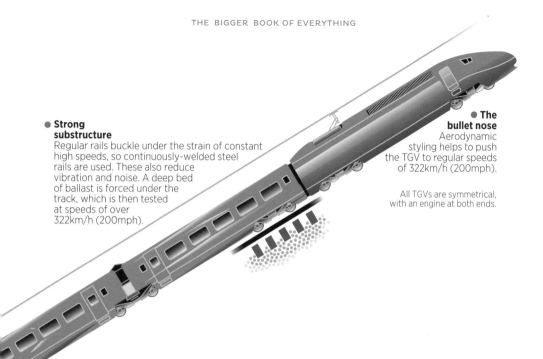

Strong substructure
Regular rails buckle under the strain of constant high speeds, so continuously-welded steel rails are used. These also reduce vibration and noise. A deep bed of ballast is forced under the track, which is then tested at speeds of over 322km/h (200mph).

The bullet nose
Aerodynamic styling helps to push the TGV to regular speeds of 322km/h (200mph).

All TGVs are symmetrical, with an engine at both ends.

WHERE FRANCE'S FAST TRAINS GO ...

to London*

Lille • Brussels

PARIS

Rennes • Le Mans Strasbourg

Tours • Dijon

— existing lines
— under construction

2 hours 10 minutes

Lyons
Valance • Turin

Bordeaux

Montpellier • Avignon • Nice

Marseille

Perpignan

250km
200 miles
both maps are the same scale

*The Eurostar is a high-speed rail service that runs through the Channel Tunnel to England. It carries 800 people in 20 cars that stretch to a total of a quarter of a mile, making it the longest passenger train in the world.

AND JAPAN'S

The first country to have a high-speed network, Japan has tested nonconventional magnetic levitation trains. The Japan Railways system is a network of Shinkansen 'bullet trains' that reach speeds of up to 320km/h (199mph).

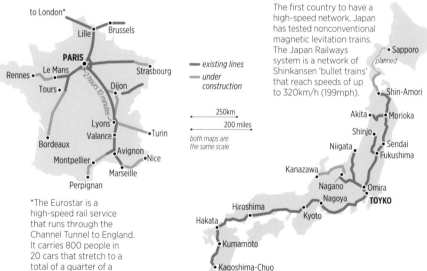

• Sapporo
planned

• Shin-Amori

Akita • • Morioka

Shinjo •

Niigata • • Sendai
• Fukushima

Kanazawa •

Nagano • • Omira
Nagoya **TOYKO**

Hiroshima •
Hakata • Kyoto

• Kumamoto

• Kagoshima-Chuo

Tunnelling under the Thames

The London Tube is the oldest underground railway system in the world. It opened in 1863 (with steam engines). All the lines were north of the river Thames—getting trains under the river was a major problem.

But Anglo-French engineer Marc Brunel (joined later by his son Isambard Kingdom Brunel) was determined to do the job. Work started in 1825, but was delayed by floods and construction failures. In 1828, the tunnel was shut down completely for 7 years.

How Brunel built his tunnel

1 A wall of **wooden boards** was placed against the bare earth.

2 An **iron structure** protected workers from falling earth and rocks.

3 The structure was braced against the tunnel face with **jacks.**

4 The boards were taken down one at a time to reveal a **sliver of earth** that was excavated to a depth of 0.3m (1ft).

5 After excavation, the board was put back in place and the next one removed. When all the boards had been taken down once and the dirt behind them dug out, the whole structure was pushed forward 0.3m (1ft). Progress was slow: just 3m (9.8ft) of tunnel was dug in a week.

The total length of the London rail system is 402km (250 miles) and 45% is underground. It's the second largest ...

Taking a walk ...

Originally intended for horse-drawn vehicles, Brunel's tunnel opened for **pedestrians** in 1843. It was 0.4km (1,300ft) long, from Wapping, in the north, to Rotherhithe, south of the river. It became a steam railway tunnel in 1869.

through the tube

The tunnel was in continuous use until an overhaul in 1995 and then another in 2007. In 2010, the tunnel once more became part of **London's urban railway system.** The nickname **"tube",** now used for the entire system, originally referred to the deep circular tunnels carrying electric trains.

Showing the way

In 1933, **Harry Beck,** an electrical engineer working for the government-run Underground Railways, conceived a new map for the system. It was a radical change from previous maps; Beck used a layout based on the electrical circuit diagrams with colour-coded lines he was used to drawing.

Because of the difficulty of showing great distances between suburban stations and short distances between stations in the centre of London (which led to a very cluttered central area), it was clearer to **ignore above-ground topography** and make the distance between all stations uniform. This resulted in a "map" that was more a diagram than a conventional map.

Beck's classic diagram has been copied by virtually all subway, bus and railway systems around the world.

rail system in the world, after Shanghai's. London's deepest station is Hampstead, at 59m (192ft) below street level.

237

How to take control of a failing jet

Would you be able to land a plane if the pilot and crew fell ill?

"These things almost land themselves, don't they?"
—Kurt Russell to Halle Berry in *Executive Decision* (1996)

Russell wasn't exactly right in that movie, but big jets do have an autopilot (and some airlines insist that their planes make an autoland every 30 days).

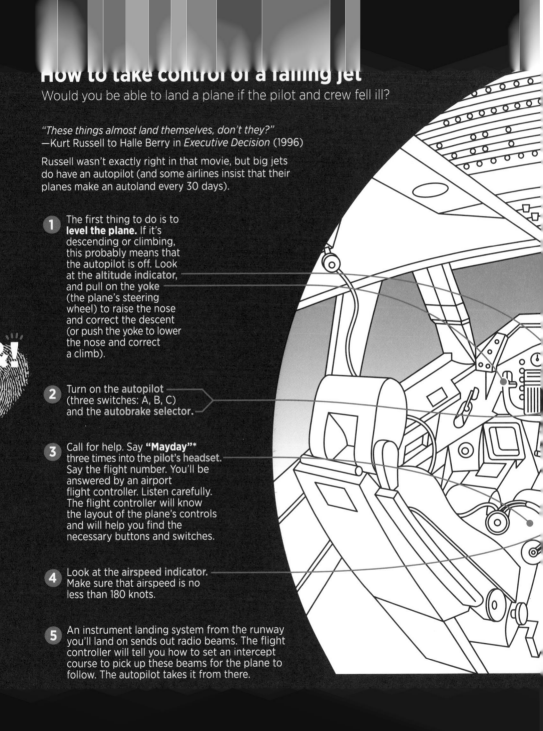

1 The first thing to do is to **level the plane.** If it's descending or climbing, this probably means that the autopilot is off. Look at the **altitude indicator,** and pull on the **yoke** (the plane's steering wheel) to raise the nose and correct the descent (or push the yoke to lower the nose and correct a climb).

2 Turn on the **autopilot** (three switches: A, B, C) and the **autobrake selector.**

3 Call for help. Say **"Mayday"*** three times into the **pilot's headset.** Say the flight number. You'll be answered by an airport flight controller. Listen carefully. The flight controller will know the layout of the plane's controls and will help you find the necessary buttons and switches.

4 Look at the **airspeed indicator.** Make sure that airspeed is no less than 180 knots.

5 An instrument landing system from the runway you'll land on sends out radio beams. The flight controller will tell you how to set an intercept course to pick up these beams for the plane to follow. The autopilot takes it from there.

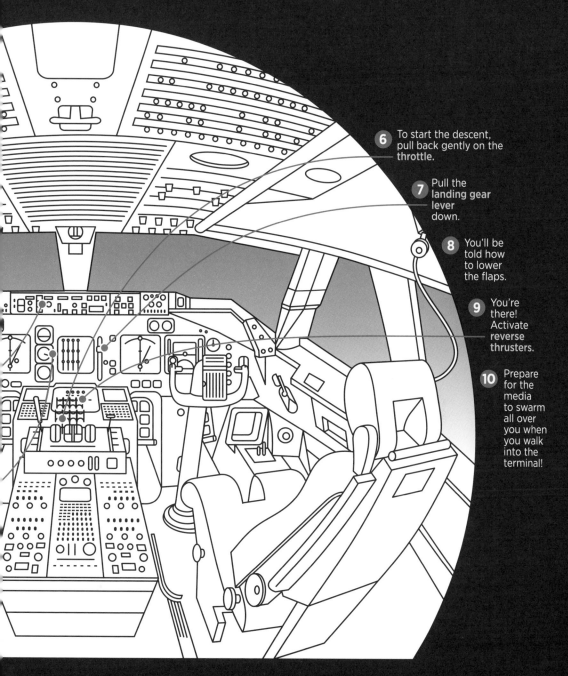

6 To start the descent, pull back gently on the **throttle.**

7 Pull the **landing gear lever** down.

8 You'll be told how to lower the flaps.

9 You're there! Activate **reverse thrusters.**

10 Prepare for the media to swarm all over you when you walk into the terminal!

Disclaimer: this is a simplified overview of the complicated landing procedure. Think hard before you volunteer!

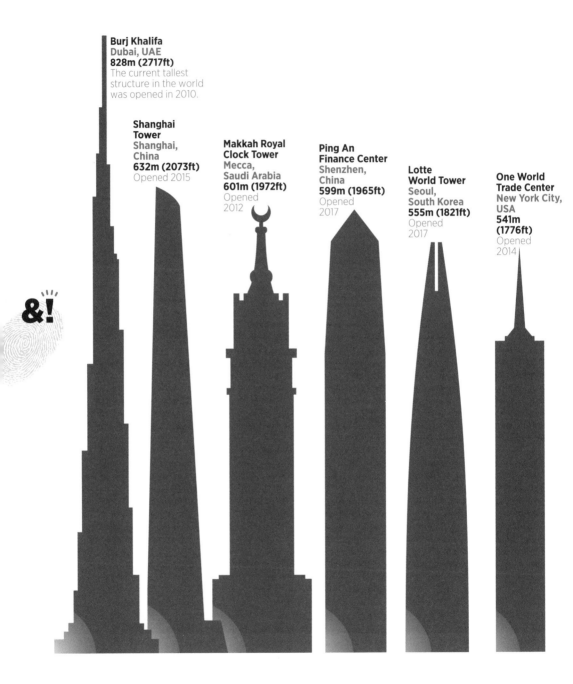

Burj Khalifa
Dubai, UAE
828m (2717ft)
The current tallest
structure in the world
was opened in 2010.

**Shanghai
Tower**
Shanghai,
China
632m (2073ft)
Opened 2015

**Makkah Royal
Clock Tower**
Mecca,
Saudi Arabia
601m (1972ft)
Opened
2012

**Ping An
Finance Center**
Shenzhen,
China
599m (1965ft)
Opened
2017

**Lotte
World Tower**
Seoul,
South Korea
555m (1821ft)
Opened
2017

**One World
Trade Center**
New York City,
USA
**541m
(1776ft)**
Opened
2014

&!

Where are the world's highest buildings?

In 2019, five of the top ten tallest buildings were in China, but don't hold your breath; **Jeddah Tower** in Saudi Arabia is projected to be finished in 2021–2022, and be **1000m (3280ft)** high.

In 1957, American architect Frank Lloyd Wright proposed a skyscraper, The Illinois, that was a mile high (1609m). It would have been twice as high as the current tallest building in the world (see left). It's said that the design of The Illinois inspired that of the Burj Khalifa.

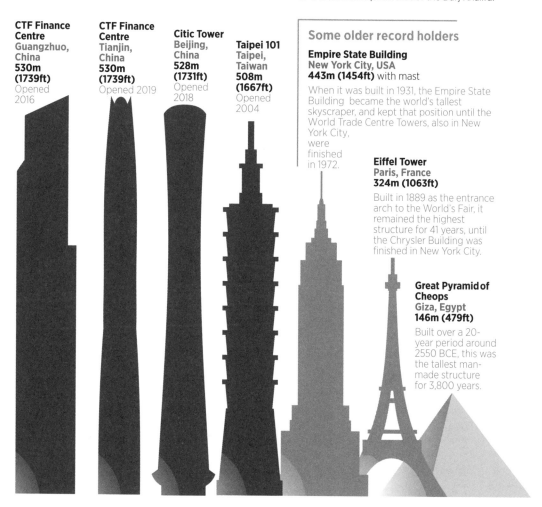

CTF Finance Centre
Guangzhuo, China
530m (1739ft)
Opened 2016

CTF Finance Centre
Tianjin, China
530m (1739ft)
Opened 2019

Citic Tower
Beijing, China
528m (1731ft)
Opened 2018

Taipei 101
Taipei, Taiwan
508m (1667ft)
Opened 2004

Some older record holders

Empire State Building
New York City, USA
443m (1454ft) with mast

When it was built in 1931, the Empire State Building became the world's tallest skyscraper, and kept that position until the World Trade Centre Towers, also in New York City, were finished in 1972.

Eiffel Tower
Paris, France
324m (1063ft)

Built in 1889 as the entrance arch to the World's Fair, it remained the highest structure for 41 years, until the Chrysler Building was finished in New York City.

Great Pyramid of Cheops
Giza, Egypt
146m (479ft)

Built over a 20-year period around 2550 BCE, this was the tallest man-made structure for 3,800 years.

What's the capital of ...?

Study this and win on quiz nights! Or perhaps you'd like to play quizmaster and see how geographically savvy your friends are.

The countries (states or territories)	Their capitals

Afghanistan	Kabul
Albania	Tirana
Algeria	Algiers
American Samoa	Pago Pago
Andorra	Andorra la Vella
Angola	Luanda
Anguilla	The Valley
Antigua & Barbuda	Saint John's
Argentina	Buenos Aires
Armenia	Yerevan
Aruba	Oranjestad
Australia	Canberra
Austria	Vienna
Azerbaijan	Baku
The Bahamas	Nassau
Bahrain	Manama
Bangladesh	Dhaka
Barbados	Bridgetown
Belarus	Minsk
Belgium	Brussels
Belize	Belmopan
Benin	Porto-Novo
Bermuda	Hamilton
Bhutan	Thimphu
Bolivia	La Paz

Bosnia & Herzegovina	Sarajevo
Botswana	Gaborone
Brazil	Brasília
Brunei	Bandar Seri Begawan
Bulgaria	Sofia
Burkina Faso	Ouagadougou
Myanmar (Burma)	Naypyidaw
Cambodia	Phnom Penh
Cameroon	Yaoundé
Canada	Ottawa
Cape Verde	Praia
Cayman Islands	George Town
Central African Rep.	Bangui
Chad	N'Djamena
Chile	Santiago
China (PRC)	Beijing
Christmas Island	Flying Fish Cove
Cocos Islands	West Island
Colombia	Bogotá
Comoros	Moroni
Congo	Brazzaville
Congo (DRC)	Kinshasa
Cook Islands	Avarua
Costa Rica	San José
Côte d'Ivoire	Yamoussoukro
Croatia	Zagreb
Cuba	Havana
Cyprus	Nicosia
Czech Republic	Prague
Denmark	Copenhagen
Djibouti	Djibouti
Dominica	Roseau
Dominican Republic	Santo Domingo
East Timor	Dili
Ecuador	Quito
Egypt	Cairo
El Salvador	San Salvador
Equatorial Guinea	Malabo
Eritrea	Asmara
Estonia	Talinn
Ethiopia	Addis Ababa
Faroe Islands	Tórshavn

Fiji	Suva
Finland	Helsinki
France	Paris
French Guiana	Cayenne
French Polynesia	Papeete
Gabon	Libreville
The Gambia	Banjul
Georgia	Tbilisi
Germany	Berlin
Ghana	Accra
Gibraltar	Gibraltar
Greece	Athens
Greenland	Nuuk
Grenada	St George's
Guadeloupe	Basse-Terre
Guam	Hagatña
Guatemala	Guatemala City
Guernsey	St Peter Port
Guinea	Conakry
Guinea-Bissau	Bissau
Guyana	Georgetown
Haiti	Port-au-Prince
Honduras	Tegucigalpa
Hungary	Budapest
Iceland	Reykjavík
India	New Delhi
Indonesia	Jakarta
Iran	Tehran
Iraq	Baghdad
Ireland	Dublin
Isle of Man	Douglas
Israel	Jerusalem
Italy	Rome
Jamaica	Kingston
Japan	Tokyo
Jersey	St Helier
Jordan	Amman
Kazakhstan	Astana
Kenya	Nairobi
Kiribati	Tarawa
Korea (North)	Pyongyang
Korea (South)	Seoul

Kosovo	**Prishtiní**	Niue	**Alofi**	South Sudan	**Juba**
Kuwait	**Kuwait City**	Norfolk Island	**Kingston**	South Ossetia	**Tskhinval**
Kyrgyzstan	**Bishkek**	Northern Mariana Islands	**Saipan**	Spain	**Madrid**
Laos	**Vientiane**	Norway	**Oslo**	Sri Lanka	**Colombo**
Latvia	**Riga**	Oman	**Muscat**	Sudan	**Khartoum**
Lebanon	**Beirut**	Pakistan	**Islamabad**	Suriname	**Paramaribo**
Lesotho	**Maseru**	Palau	**Ngerulmud**	Svalbard	**Longyearbyen**
Liberia	**Monrovia**	Palestine	**Ramallah and Gaza**	Swaziland	**Mbabane**
Libya	**Tripoli**	Panama	**Panama City**	Sweden	**Stockholm**
Liechtenstein	**Vaduz**	Papua New Guinea	**Port Moresby**	Switzerland	**Bern**
Lithuania	**Vilnius**	Paraguay	**Asunción**	Syria	**Damascus**
Luxembourg	**Luxembourg City**	Peru	**Lima**	Taiwan	**Taipei**
North Macedonia	**Skopje**	Philippines	**Manila**	Tajikistan	**Dushanbe**
Madagascar	**Antananarivo**	Pitcairn Islands	**Adamstown**	Tanzania	**Dodoma**
Malawi	**Lilongwe**	Poland	**Warsaw**	Thailand	**Bangkok**
Malaysia	**Kuala Lumpur**	Portugal	**Lisbon**	Togo	**Lomé**
Maldives	**Malé**	Puerto Rico	**San Juan**	Tokelau	(None)
Mali	**Bamako**	Qatar	**Doha**	Tonga	**Nuku'alofa**
Malta	**Valletta**	Réunion	**Saint-Denis**	Trinidad & Tobago	**Port of Spain**
Marshall Islands	**Majuro**	Romania	**Bucharest**	Tunisia	**Tunis**
Martinique	**Fort-de-France**	Russia	**Moscow**	Turkey	**Ankara**
Mauritania	**Nouakchott**	Rwanda	**Kigali**	Turkish Rep. of N. Cyprus	**Nicosia**
Mauritius	**Port Louis**	St-Pierre and Miquelon	**Saint-Pierre**	Turkmenistan	**Ashgabat**
Mayotte	**Mamoudzou**	St Helena	**Jamestown**	Turks & Caicos Islands	**Cockburn Town**
Mexico	**Mexico City**	St Kitts and Nevis	**Basseterre**	Tuvalu	**Fongafale**
Fed. States of Micronesia	**Palikir**	St Lucia	**Castries**	Uganda	**Kampala**
Moldova	**Chisinau**	St Vincent & the Grenadines	**Kingstown**	Ukraine	**Kiev**
Monaco	**Monaco**	Samoa	**Apia**	UAE	**Abu Dhabi**
Mongolia	**Ulaanbaatar**	San Marino	**San Marino**	UK	**London**
Montenegro	**Podgorica**	São Tomé & Príncipe	**São Tomé**	USA	**Washington, DC**
Montserrat	**Brades Estate**	Saudi Arabia	**Riyadh**	Uruguay	**Montevideo**
Morocco	**Rabat**	Senegal	**Dakar**	Uzbekistan	**Tashkent**
Mozambique	**Maputo**	Serbia	**Belgrade**	Vanuatu	**Port Vila**
Namibia	**Windhoek**	Seychelles	**Victoria**	Vatican City	**Vatican City**
Nauru	**Yaren**	Sierra Leone	**Freetown**	Venezuela	**Caracas**
Nepal	**Kathmandu**	Singapore	**Singapore**	Vietnam	**Hanoi**
Netherlands	**Amsterdam**	Slovakia	**Bratislava**	British Virgin Is.	**Road Town**
New Caledonia	**Nouméa**	Slovenia	**Ljubljana**	US Virgin Islands	**Charlotte Amalie**
New Zealand	**Wellington**	Solomon Islands	**Honiara**	Wallis & Futuna	**Mata'Utu**
Nicaragua	**Managua**	Somalia	**Mogadishu**	Yemen	**Sana'a**
Niger	**Niamey**	South Africa	**Pretoria**	Zambia	**Lusaka**
Nigeria	**Abuja**		(administrative capital); **Cape Town** (legislative capital); **Bloemfontein** (judicial capital)	Zimbabwe	**Harare**

How to choose a diamond

Most diamonds, the transparent form of pure carbon, are 3 billion years old.
They are the oldest things you'll ever own.

If you are planning to propose on a romantic holiday getaway,
here is some information you might like to know about "a girl's best friend".

(1) **Can it get scratches?** No. The Mohs scale (invented in 1812 to measure the hardness of minerals) shows that nothing will scratch a diamond.

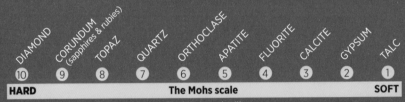

DIAMOND	CORUNDUM (sapphires & rubies)	TOPAZ	QUARTZ	ORTHOCLASE	APATITE	FLUORITE	CALCITE	GYPSUM	TALC
10	9	8	7	6	5	4	3	2	1

HARD　　　　The Mohs scale　　　　**SOFT**

Each mineral will
scratch everything below it on the scale,
but not the ones above it.

&!

(2) **What are the "4 Cs"?** Experts consider these factors when rating a diamond:

CARAT
This is the
weight of
the stone.

CLARITY
This refers to
inclusions (flaws)
in the stone; the
fewer the better.

COLOUR
This is the
degree to which
the stone is
colourless. (You
want as little
colour as
possible.)

CUT ☞
The stone's
angles and
proportions.

(3) So what's the
difference
between a
carat and a
karat?

Funny you
should ask.
It's all right
here.

A **carat** is a unit
of weight for
precious gems.
One carat = 200ml
(0.007oz).

At that rate, your
precious 5.4kg
(12lb) cat is a
27,216-carat pet!

A **karat** is a unit of
purity for gold.
Pure gold is 24-
karat, but it's too
soft to make
jewellery. So a ring
that is 18-karat
gold has six parts
of some other
metal mixed in.

What's the ideal cut? The form shown here, incorporating 58 facets, was developed in 1919 to maximise reflection of light from the interior of the diamond, making it appear to sparkle.

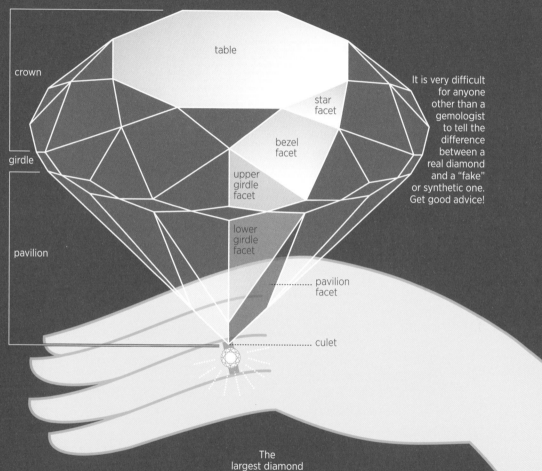

crown

table

star facet

bezel facet

upper girdle facet

lower girdle facet

girdle

pavilion

pavilion facet

culet

It is very difficult for anyone other than a gemologist to tell the difference between a real diamond and a "fake" or synthetic one. Get good advice!

The largest diamond ever found was the **3106.7-carat Cullinan.** Discovered in South Africa in 1905, it was later cut into nine separate stones. One of those, Cullinan 1, or the **Great Star of Africa,** was the largest polished diamond in the world (530.2 carats) until the discovery of the Golden Jubilee Diamond (545.7 carats) in the same mine in 1985.

The Great Star of Africa is part of the Crown Jewels of the UK.

On the road: what do those signs mean?

Seven of the signals a motorcycle leader makes to riders behind.
They are all made with the left hand.

turn left
palm down

turn right
fist clenched

slow down
palm down

go faster
is the same
but with palm
facing up

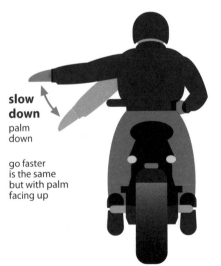

stop
palm facing back

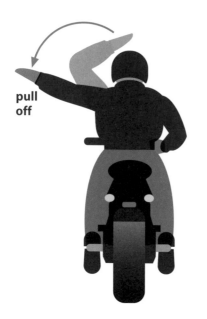

pull off

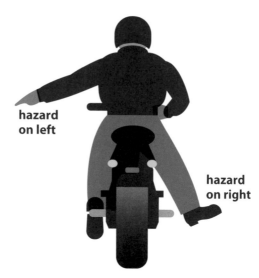

hazard on left

hazard on right

police ahead
tap helmet

The bikers' salute is a greeting that's customarily returned by other motor-cyclists.

two fingers:
I'm riding a 2-cylinder bike

four:
4-cylinder bike

Riding a camel

One hump or two? If you are planning to view the pyramids on camelback, you'll most likely be on a **one-humped dromedary,** or Arabian camel.*

1 **Camels are mean,** they spit and they smell, but once you are up there you'll want to take pictures. Beware, because you're in for a **bumpy ride** and it's a long way down to the sand if you drop your camera, so make sure it's tethered to you.

2 **Choose the right clothing**

● A **hat** with a chinstrap and a flap at the back that covers your neck will keep the sun at bay.

● Put your **sunglasses** on.

● Roll your **sleeves** down, or slather your arms with sunscreen.

● Tie a **windbreaker** around your waist.

● Wear **baggy, long trousers.** Tuck them into your socks. (Camel hair is scratchy.)

● Camels don't walk smoothly, so flip-flops will come off easily. **Wear boots or shoes.**

Make friends! Camels like carrots and apples.

3 Make sure the animal is either **securely tied** with a rope or is being held by its owner.

● Everything will get dirty and smelly, so **washable clothes that dry fast** are best.

● Be **respectful of local culture.** Women should not wear skimpy clothing. (Besides, the sun will punish you if you do!)

*The **two-humped Bactrian camel** is found wild in the steppes of Central Asia, where there are only about 1000 left. There's a greater number of domesticated Bactrian camels living in Asia, but they are also on official endangered animals lists. You can ride them, snuggled between the humps.

4

Getting on

The "saddle" is a series of pads arranged around the hump, ending up as a flat platform. There might be either a stirrup or a small ledge attached to this to help you climb aboard. But if you are lucky, the camel guide will provide a **footstool, or small stepladder,** which makes mounting much easier.

5

Standing on the stepladder, swing your right leg over the seat in **one smooth movement.** Don't hesitate! Grip the front handle with one hand and the back handle with the other.

6

Be confident— the camel will sense if you aren't.

7

Camels get up with their back legs first. This is scary: **lean back on the seat.**

8

When they raise their front legs, **lean forward.**

9

Unlike most animals, when camels walk, they lift both their front and back left legs at the same time. Then they lift both front and back legs on the right side. This makes for a **weird swaying motion.** Just go with it!

10

Watch seasoned riders. They **lift both knees to a 90-degree bend,** rather than straddling the seat as you would on a horse.

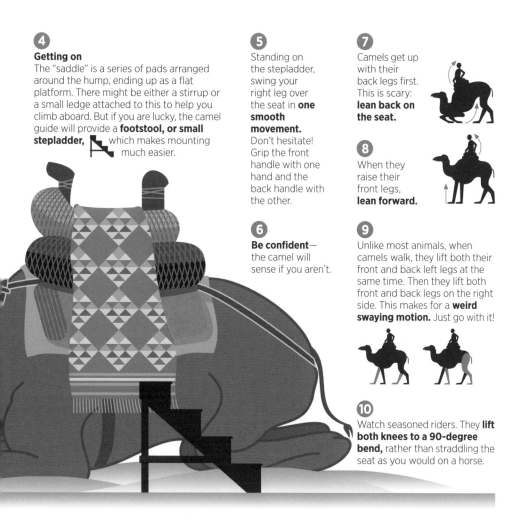

Thousand of camels were introduced into **Australia** in the 1800s. When motorised vehicles replaced the camels' transport role in the 20th century, many were released into the wild. There are now **more than a million** feral camels in Australia. Most are dromedaries, originally from India and North Africa, while a lesser number of Bactrians came from China and Mongolia.

Hey, Mum, Dad, why ...?

Knowing how to answer kids' questions will help pass the time on a long road trip.

Here, their questions are all about **colours.**

Why is the sky blue?

1 Thirty-two kilometres (20 miles) above the Earth, the sky is black.

2 "White" light from the sun is **all colours** of the rainbow.

3 About 29km (18 miles) up, the light meets **air molecules (O).**

4 Light at the **violet** end is scattered more than the rest of the spectrum.

5 **This light** is scattered from one molecule to the next so violet light should dominate, then blue, etc.

6 But we see the sky as **blue** because our eyes are better at seeing blue than violet.

Why are clouds white?

1 Cloud droplets are much bigger than air molecules, so they scatter **all** the colours of sunlight.

This effectively makes the light appear **white** as the colours are scattered through the clouds.

Why is the sunset red?

1 At sunset (and sunrise), light from the sun is travelling **farther** through the atmosphere.

2 This means that more light at the blue end of the spectrum is scattered, leaving the **red, orange and yellow** for us to see.

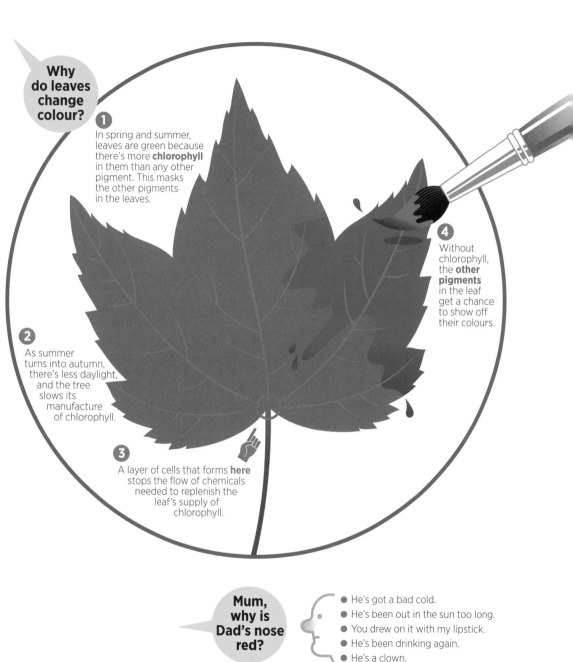

Why do leaves change colour?

1 In spring and summer, leaves are green because there's more **chlorophyll** in them than any other pigment. This masks the other pigments in the leaves.

2 As summer turns into autumn, there's less daylight, and the tree slows its manufacture of chlorophyll.

3 A layer of cells that forms **here** stops the flow of chemicals needed to replenish the leaf's supply of chlorophyll.

4 Without chlorophyll, the **other pigments** in the leaf get a chance to show off their colours.

Mum, why is Dad's nose red?

- He's got a bad cold.
- He's been out in the sun too long.
- You drew on it with my lipstick.
- He's been drinking again.
- He's a clown.

Sketching on holiday

It doesn't matter if you think you can't draw; just try it! The memories of your trips are so much better when you have painted them (or just scribbled something in pencil). Keep a visual diary. Years later, you'll wow yourself with stuff you had forgotten.

You don't need a lot of art materials. In fact, the fewer the better: if you give yourself too many choices, you'll never get going.

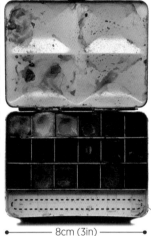

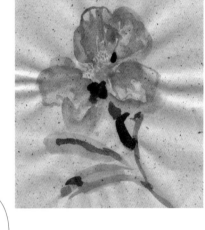

A flower in our hotel room. You can **use any kind of paper** that's around. (If it's cheap and thin like this, from a notebook made of recycled paper, the water might crinkle the page a bit, but who cares? The rock rose is preserved!

⟵ 8cm (3in) ⟶

This little **watercolour** box came with its own brush (in a travel tube that doubles as a handle). You just need a little water bottle, and off you go!

The view across the river from a friend's house.

Sometimes it's inconvenient to paint—a simple **pen or pencil** will do.

These seaside bathers don't have to know you are drawing them!

Drawing in nightclubs is a challenge; you can't really see what you are doing. But don't fret over any "wrong" lines you might make. As jazz pianist Thelonious Monk said when people criticised him for what sounded like mistakes in his playing, "there are no wrong notes in music". It's the same when you try to sketch a live performance: your wobbly attempts to capture a musician's intensity can add an in-the-moment reality to the drawing. This is Kurt Rosenwinkel at the Village Vanguard, in New York City.

TUESDAY, JULY 13, 2010.

These quick sketches of seagulls were done on newspaper. It's a terrific surface to draw on; don't leave it in the sun, though, it will go yellow surprisingly quickly.

Southport Beach
7/13
/10

Never mind; accidents happen.

Details, details

Sure, you'll take lots of snapshots of your friends in front of the Eiffel Tower, or the Taj Mahal, the pyramids or the Sydney Opera House, but don't overlook the colourful, sometimes abstract snippets of fun under your feet, on walls or on your dinner plate.

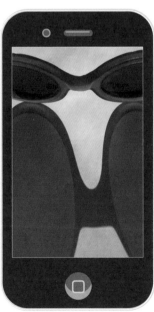

No special effects or filters here. All the pictures were taken with a basic mobile phone camera.

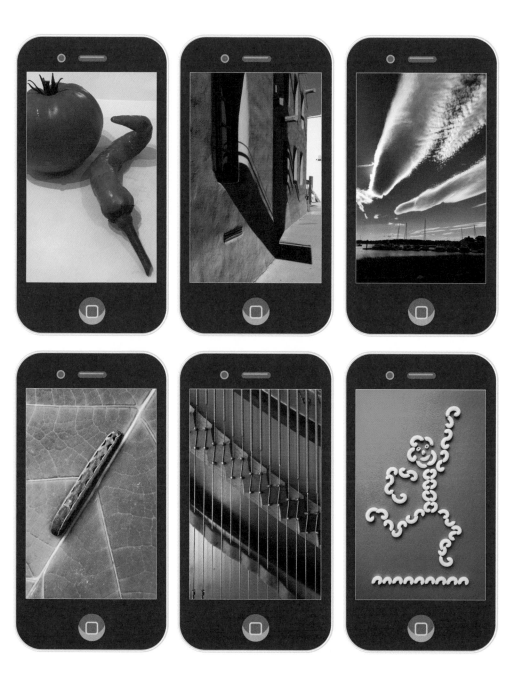

Going batty

Bats account for about one-fifth of all mammals on Earth (and they are the only mammals that can fly). There are almost 1000 species, and they can be found on every continent except Antarctica.

This is an insect-eating **Mexican free-tailed bat.** It's fairly small—this drawing is life-sized—but some fruit-eating bats have wingspans of 1.5m (5ft).

Some places to see bats

Free-tailed bats are found in **southwestern USA, Mexico, Central America and northern parts of South America.**

About 20,000 **rosetta fruit bats** live in **Buoyem Sacred Groves, in Ghana.**

The London Bat Group arranges evening walks in many **London parks,** where you can see **pipistrelles, noctules, serotines and Daubenton's.**

Spandau Citadel in Berlin is known to have been the haunt of **many species of bats** for centuries. The Citadel is a renaissance military fort built from 1559 to 1594.

Also in Germany, near **Bad Segeberg,** is the **Noctalis bat exhibition** and the nearby **Kalkberg bat cave,** where thousands of **Daubenton's** and **Natterer's** bats come to hibernate every winter.

About 90 species of bat have a **free tail** that extends beyond the flap of skin between their legs.

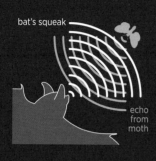

bat's squeak

echo from moth

Radar

When hunting for food, most bats send out a series of high-pitched squeaks, which bounce off any object in their path, producing an echo that's picked up by the bat's sensitive ears.

Bat myths exposed!

(By talking bats, no less.)

I hate the phrase "blind as a bat". Our eyesight is not bad at all. I mean, sometimes we don't even send out radar squeaks.

I know! Very few bats contract rabies, and we die from it, we don't fly around! And we never bite humans, unless it's in self-defence.

The wings are a leathery, elastic membrane stretched over elongated forearms. Long finger bones support the tips of the wing membrane.

Vampires

Ever since Bram Stoker included blood-drinking vampire bats in his *Dracula* novel, they've made regular creepy appearances in horror films and books.

Vampire bats are found in Mexico, Brazil, Chile and Argentina, but not Transylvania!

Vampire bats' entire food supply is blood. They need 2 tablespoons a day and if they go 2 nights without it, they starve to death.

Vampire bats don't suck blood from their prey, but they do bite. An anticoagulant in their saliva keeps the victim's blood flowing.

Draculin, a drug developed from this anticoagulant is being tested as a treatment for stroke patients.

If the world were ruled by cats ...

They'd redesign national flags, so the rest of us would understand that they are in charge. (These new flags are not presented in alphabetical order, because cats don't care about things like that.)

The cat flag of
Sweden

The cat flag of
Japan

The cat flag of
India

The cat flag of
São Tomé and Principé

The cat flag of
Saudi Arabia

The cat flag of
South Korea

The cat flag of
Nepal

The cat flag of
Australia

The cat flag of
Italy

The cat flag of
Papua New Guinea

The cat flag of
China

The cat flag of
Senegal

The cat flag of
Brazil

The cat flag of
Canada

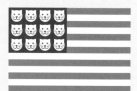

The cat flag of
the USA

The cat flag of
Switzerland

The cat flag of
Sri Lanka

The cat flag of
Mauritania

Get wet!

Even if you know how to swim, this will help you to be a better, faster **aquatic athlete.** (And you can call yourself that when you want to show off.)

1 **Kick efficiently: don't let your feet rise above the water line**

This maximises the effort you put into kicking, and minimises drag. (see 2, below.)

&!

2 **Streamline your body to decrease drag**

You can do this by keeping the body horizontal in the water, and not letting your backside and legs drift downwards. This is called balancing the body.

3 **Instead of swimming on your stomach, roll from side to side with each stroke**

By doing this you'll be presenting a slimmer profile and less resistance to the water, enabling you to glide through it like a fish. And you'll be using the core muscles of your back, hips and torso to apply more force to the stroke.

4 Swim "taller"

Using the principle that a longer, tapered vessel glides through water more easily and faster than a shorter one, reach out as far as you can with each stroke, and leave your hand there longer before retracting to start the next stroke.

5 Keep your head and eyes down

Bringing your head up works against the effort of keeping the body in a straight line—it unbalances you.

6 OK, so you have to breathe!

Raise your head slightly, when you have rolled to one side or the other, to grab a quick breath.

7 Keep your fingers slightly open ...

not tight together nor wide apart. A separation actually makes a web of water between the fingers, giving you more "pull."

How to toss a caber

Scotland's Highland games
are held in many locations throughout
the year to celebrate Scottish and
Celtic culture. One of the "heavy"
competitions, **tossing the caber,**
has come to symbolize the
whole gathering.

The caber (from the
Gaelic word for a
wooden beam) is
typically made
from a larch
tree. It's 5.94m
(19.5ft) long
and weighs
79kg
(175lb).

The sport is
thought to have
been developed
from tossing logs
across ditches to
make a bridge.

&!

1

The competitor
balances the caber
on his shoulder
(with the help of
friends) and starts
a short run forward,
keeping the pole
balanced in front of
him. (Not as easy as
you might think
given its weight
and length.)

2

He stops and lets
the caber swing
forward.

3

Lifting the caber
as high as he
can, he thrusts
it up into
the air.

They toss cabers in other countries, too!
Worldwide Highland games

CANADA
Calgary, Alberta
and some 25 other
Canadian gatherings
during May, June,
July and August.

USA
Pleasanton, CA
and at about 30
other locations
around the
country.

BERMUDA
Somerset

BRAZIL
Rio Grande do Sul

Scotland

England

SCOTLAND
The Cowal Games, Dunoon
Held every August, this is the largest
Highland games gathering in the world.
There are at least 10 other major
annual gatherings in Scotland.

HUNGARY
Csesznek

SWITZERLAND
Abtwil, St. Gallen

INDONESIA
Jakarta

NEW ZEALAND
Waipu

As well as tossing the caber,
Highland games gatherings include the
Scottish hammer throw, various weight throws,
and the stone put (much the same as the
Olympic shot put).

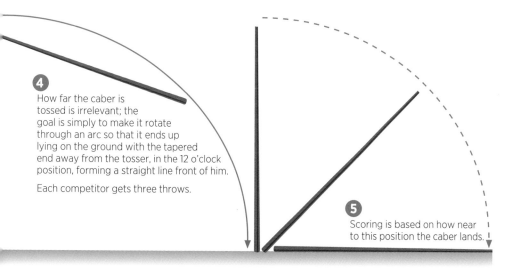

4
How far the caber is
tossed is irrelevant; the
goal is simply to make it rotate
through an arc so that it ends up
lying on the ground with the tapered
end away from the tosser, in the 12 o'clock
position, forming a straight line front of him.

Each competitor gets three throws.

5
Scoring is based on how near
to this position the caber lands.

Fast on ice

Like many sports, speedskating has taken advantage of technology. Top skaters use **clap skates** to compete in world-class events.

Clap skates were invented by the Dutch around 2000. Not coincidentally, athletes from the Netherlands hold many world records in the sport.

1 The **clap skate** allows the edge of a blade to remain in full contact with the ice for an extra moment, even though the foot is beginning to lift off.

2 The brief added contact with the ice means that a skater can exert more force on the blade, which in turn generates **more speed.**

Under the ice, pipes containing **liquid refrigerant** are embedded in a perfectly flat cement floor.

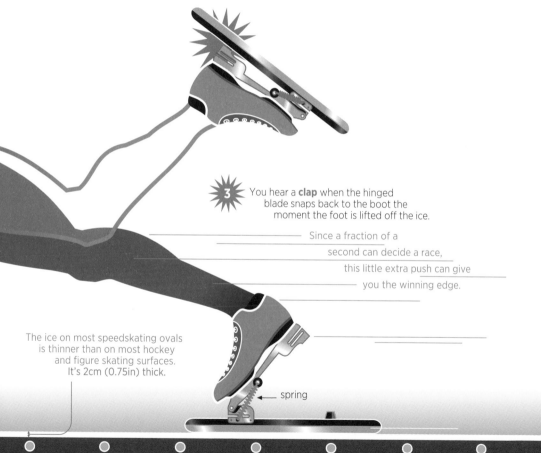

3 You hear a **clap** when the hinged blade snaps back to the boot the moment the foot is lifted off the ice.

Since a fraction of a second can decide a race, this little extra push can give you the winning edge.

The ice on most speedskating ovals is thinner than on most hockey and figure skating surfaces. It's 2cm (0.75in) thick.

spring

A computer using temperature data from **sensors that are built into the slab** (and suspended above the ice) warms or cools the refrigerant to keep the surface temperature between -9.4°C (15°F) and -7.8°C (18°F).

265

Be an origamist! Yes, it's a word.

Origami comes from the Japanese *ori*, meaning folding, and *kami,* paper. Known since the 1600s, the goal is to fold a square of paper—often with a different colour on the back—into (usually) a bird or an animal. Strict origamists say no glue, no cutting.

Basic folds

Almost all origami pieces start with a combination of these simple folds.

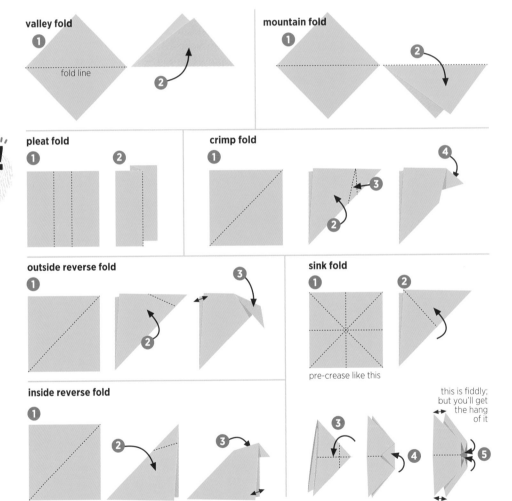

valley fold

fold line

mountain fold

pleat fold

crimp fold

outside reverse fold

sink fold

pre-crease like this

this is fiddly; but you'll get the hang of it

inside reverse fold

Something for a long plane ride: folding a blue and yellow crane

Use paper that's about 18cm (7in) square.

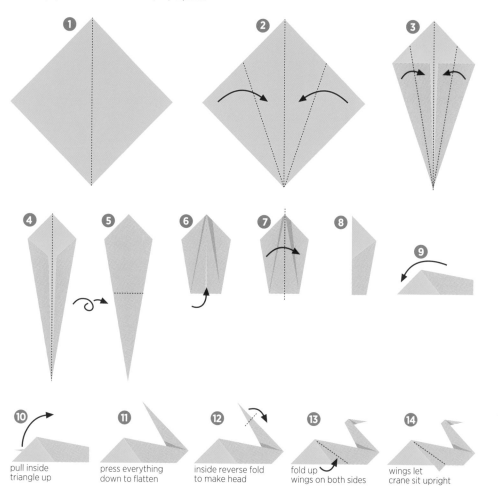

10 pull inside triangle up

11 press everything down to flatten

12 inside reverse fold to make head

13 fold up wings on both sides

14 wings let crane sit upright

The finished crane should look something like this (here using plain white paper).

Don't worry if your first attempt doesn't quite work. It takes time to become an expert!

Inside a Formula 1 car

Wait, that's the steering wheel? Better study up before driving it at 200mph (322kph).

Bird's eye view of an F1 car ...   **and how you control it**

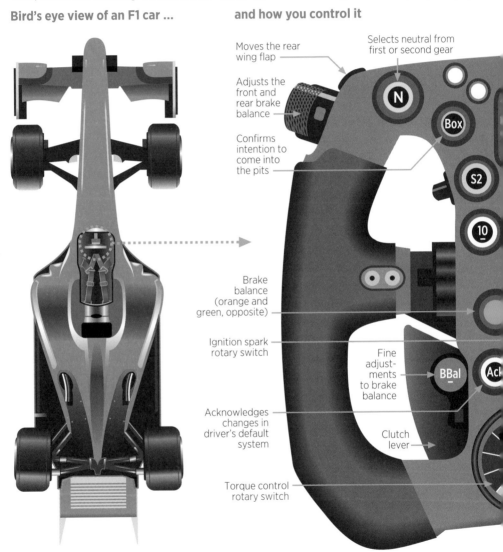

Moves the rear wing flap

Adjusts the front and rear brake balance

Confirms intention to come into the pits

Selects neutral from first or second gear

Brake balance (orange and green, opposite)

Ignition spark rotary switch

Fine adjustments to brake balance

Acknowledges changes in driver's default system

Clutch lever

Torque control rotary switch

N

Box

S2

10

BBal

Ac

This is a simplified version of the steering wheel in Sauber F1 team cars (renamed Alfa Romeo Racing for 2019).

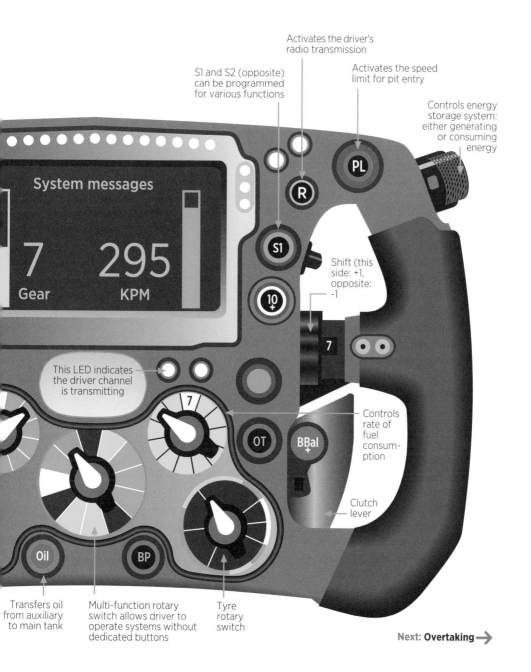

Activates the driver's
radio transmission

Activates the speed
limit for pit entry

S1 and S2 (opposite)
can be programmed
for various functions

Controls energy
storage system:
either generating
or consuming
energy

System messages

7 295

Gear KPM

R

PL

S1

10
+

Shift (this
side: +1,
opposite:
-1

7

This LED indicates
the driver channel
is transmitting

7

OT

BBal
+

Controls
rate of
fuel
consum-
ption

Clutch
lever

Oil

BP

Transfers oil
from auxiliary
to main tank

Multi-function rotary
switch allows driver to
operate systems without
dedicated buttons

Tyre
rotary
switch

Next: **Overtaking** →

How to overtake

① Slipstreaming

The red car acts as a battering ram, punching through the air in front of it. This reduces the air pressure in front of the blue car, allowing its engine to work less while keeping the same speed.

Blue follows close behind red, waiting for the opportunity to duck out and overtake on the inside.

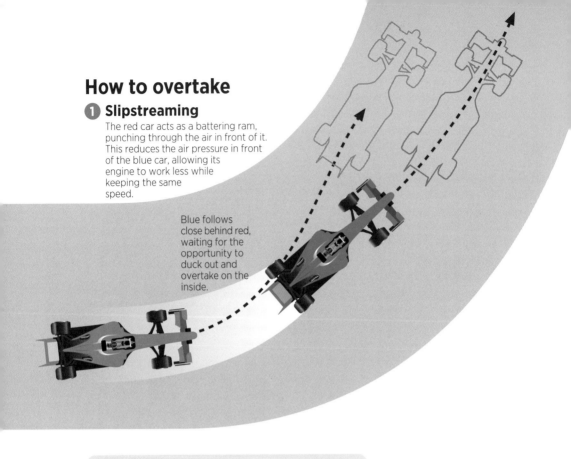

What the signalling flags mean

When a signal is intended for one particular car, a sign with the car's number accompanies the flag.

Dangerous situation on the track—
no overtaking

Slippery track—
slow down

Slow vehicle on track (such as an ambulance)—
slow down

Race stopped
because of extreme danger

When waved: you are **about to be lapped— must let car pass**

② Out-braking

Approaching a corner, blue waits longer to brake than red, forcing red to take a wider, slower line.

But there's no room for blue to miscalculate: if it goes through the turn too quickly, it could end up on the outside of the track, allowing red to cross back to the inside—retaking the lead.

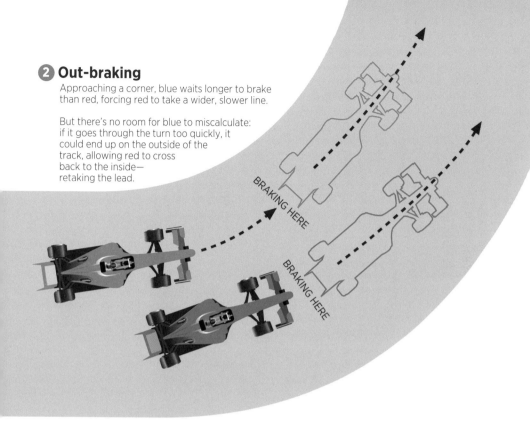

BRAKING HERE

BRAKING HERE

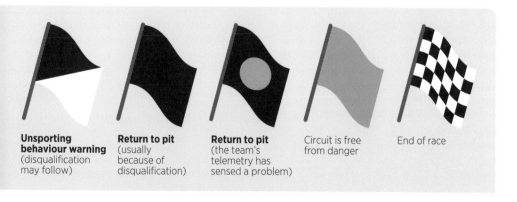

Unsporting behaviour warning (disqualification may follow)

Return to pit (usually because of disqualification)

Return to pit (the team's telemetry has sensed a problem)

Circuit is free from danger

End of race

Cheese rolling!

Really. They do it in England.

Cheese rolling has taken place in England since the 15th century.

The modern event is held every spring at Cooper's Hill, Brockhurst, in Gloucestershire.

1 Foolhardy contestants line up.

2 The **Official Roller** pushes the cheese down the hill, with a second or two head start before the runners go.

3 This part of the hill is not visible from the top.

4 The cheese is a **Double Gloucester** wheel weighing 4kg (9lb).

International cheese rollers!

It's not just another totally English oddity; in 2019 a Canadian won one of the races. And in the past, Japanese and American contestants have won races.

5 As the cheese rolls down the hill it can reach **112km/h (70mph).** Because of the danger to spectators, it was replaced by a foam replica in 2013.

6 There are **four downhill races** (three for men, one for women) and uphill races for boys and girls under 14 (no cheese involved).

If cheese throwing isn't silly enough for you, try

Rat throwing!
Really. They do it in Spain.

In the centuries-old tradition of **San Pedro Nolasco,** people in El Puig smash *cuañas,* which are like piñatas, but made of clay. Half of the *cuañas* are filled with dead rats, the rest with candy. The rats are then thrown at the crowd. A *Batalla de Ratas* ensues.

Madrid
El Puig
Valencia

Not content with hurling **dead rats,** which is officially banned but still takes place every January, Spaniards also have festivals for throwing:

flour & eggs
tomatoes
black tar
flowers
grapes
water

6 **The winner** is the first person to reach the finish line. The prize: a Double Gloucester cheese wheel. (A real one, not the foam version they chased!)

7 **Ambulances** wait to ferry injured runners to the local hospital. There are several accidents every year.

185m (200yd) from start to finish

Building sand castles

Your first effort will probably collapse. Don't worry!

Getting ready

1 The right stuff

The best sand for sculpting is fine. Pick up some wet sand, squeeze it into a golf ball-sized blob and roll it around in your hand. If it stays in one piece, it'll be good for building.

2 What time is high tide?

And how far does it reach up the beach? Get the local tide tables. It's a pity when your work is washed away.

3 Essential equipment

Shovel
full-length handle, small scoop

Compacting buckets see ↗

Sculpting tools
kitchen spatulas, etc

Heavy piece of wood
for compacting

Water spray bottle
keeps sand damp

Water buckets

4 Bring a picture

Inspiration—something to work from. Not all castles look alike. Besides, who said you have to build a castle? How about a car? Or an animal? A giant hot dog? (Why not?)

Compaction is the key

5 Make building blocks

Remove the handle and lid from your compacting bucket.
The best type to use is a plastic 19L (5 gall) with straight sides.

Flip it over and cut a hole in the bottom.

On the beach, shovel in about 10cm (4in) wet sand; add water.

Pack the sand down hard with the wood block. Repeat with sand and water until the cylinder is full.

Tap sides of bucket and lift up.

A perfect compacted building block!

Sculpting

6 Work from the top down

That way the scraped away sand will not fall on work you've already done.

7 Keep edges crisp

Carve in towards the centre of a shape from both sides (if you drag a sculpting tool through a shape, the outside edge tends to fall away).

8 Making windows

Outline the shape first, then cut into the center to get rid of sand, and only then go in to make the edges neat and sharp.

Buying a carpet

It might not be a magic one, but it'll certainly be beautiful. Experts consider the very best oriental rugs to be Persian. The world's oldest-known example is the Persian Pazyryk carpet, which was discovered in 1949. Carbon dating indicates that it was woven in the 5th century BCE.

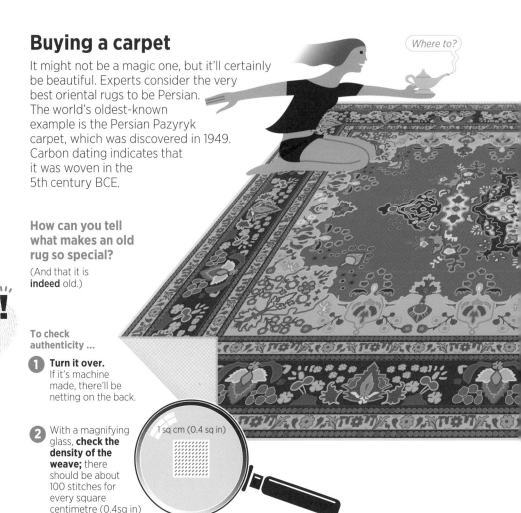

Where to?

How can you tell what makes an old rug so special?

(And that it is **indeed** old.)

To check authenticity ...

1 **Turn it over.** If it's machine made, there'll be netting on the back.

2 With a magnifying glass, **check the density of the weave;** there should be about 100 stitches for every square centimetre (0.4sq in)

1 sq cm (0.4 sq in)

3 Ask to **burn** an unpicked knot or snippet of fringe; silk and wool smoulder, their substitutes catch alight.

4 **Examine the colour.** The best oriental rugs use natural dyes from vegetables and other sources. You can spot artificial dyes by looking for colours that are markedly stronger than others. Anything orange or pink indicates a manmade rug.

And inspect the weave. The colour in artificial dyes is consistent all the way from the base of the thread to the tip. Natural dyes are more patchy.

Design: abstract symbols or pictures of real things?

Often, motifs are derived from **plants** found in the area where the carpet was made. One of the most common is a twisted teardrop known as the 'boteh'. It's of Persian origin, but the English-speaking world knows it by another name, after it was brought back by colonists: **paisley.**

Modern Afghan war rugs incorporate distinctly untraditional motifs: helicopters and guns.

Know the market

Iran produces about 13 million sq km (5 million sq miles) of carpets annually, and exports them to more than 100 countries. (Hand-woven rugs are one of its main non-oil export items.)

Savvy buyers **avoid the big carpet manufacturing towns** on this map, and head to hidden corners of Iran, Turkey and Syria to find the best deals.

The **most expensive carpet** in the world is a 17th-century Persian rug that was auctioned in London for £21.8m ($33.8m) in 2013.

Sax appeal

Adolphe Sax invented the saxophone in the early 1840s.*
At first it was made of wood, and was played mostly
by French army bands. In a couple of years,
Monsieur Sax started to use brass
to make his instruments. In the
1920s, clarinetist Sidney Bechet
took up the sax, and it's
been a staple of jazz
ever since.

For some jazz inspiration,
listen to the music of
Charlie Parker, drawn here.
Parker was arguably the
saxophone's finest and
most original player.
While his finger
movements were
mechanical, his
music was art.
It'll take time, and
some awful squeaks,
but with practice,
you can make
art too. Or at
least, better
squeaks.

1 Blow into the mouthpiece, causing a bamboo reed to vibrate.

2 The vibrating column of air travels down the instrument's cone-shaped tube.

3 You operate a system of levers to open and close holes on the tube.

4 When you leave the holes **open**, a **high note** is produced.

When you move the levers to **close** the holes, **lower notes** are produced.

*Adolphe Sax also invented
the saxotromba, the saxhorn,
and the saxtuba. Just thought
you'd like to know.

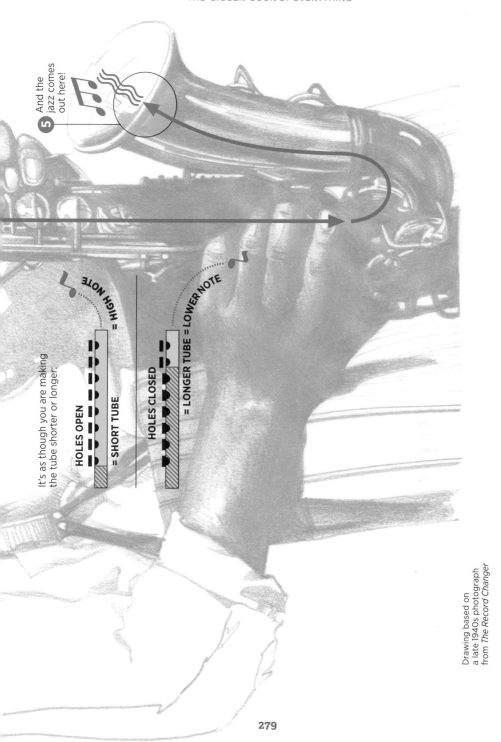

5 And the jazz comes out here!

It's as though you are making the tube shorter or longer.

HOLES OPEN = SHORT TUBE = HIGH NOTE

HOLES CLOSED = LONGER TUBE = LOWER NOTE

Drawing based on a late 1940s photograph from *The Record Changer*

Starry, starry night

It's been a long day on the trail. Back at your campsite, lie down and gaze at the night sky. Are we alone, or is there anyone else out there?

Thinking about extraterrestrial life ...   and looking at ...

A few years ago, astronomers at the University of California, Berkeley SETI* Research Center made a presentation to the US Congress about the possibility of other life in space.

Perhaps it's time to say goodbye to Earth, and extend our travel plans a bit!

&!

THE SETI PRESENTATION INCLUDED:

★ 2000 exoplanets have been discovered in the last 20 years, thanks to the Kepler space telescopes.

★ 70% of all stars are accompanied by planets, so there could be one trillion planets in the Milky Way. (And the Milky Way is only one of the 150 billion galaxies visible to our telescopes.)

M I L K Y   W A Y

★ If just one star in five has a habitable planet orbiting it, the Milky way could be home to anywhere from 10 billion to 80 billion Earth-lke planets

★ **The possibility of extraterrestrial lfe is "close to 100 percent".**

★ "The chance of finding [life] ... will happen in the next 20 years depending on the financing".

*Search for Extraterrestrial Intelligence

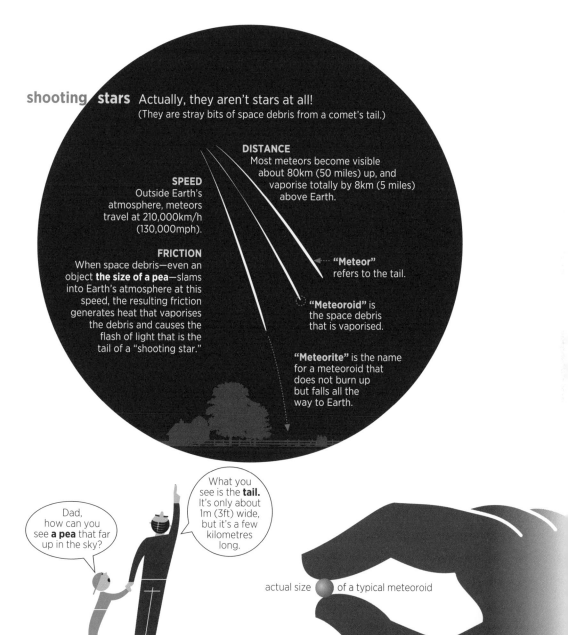

shooting stars Actually, they aren't stars at all!
(They are stray bits of space debris from a comet's tail.)

DISTANCE
Most meteors become visible about 80km (50 miles) up, and vaporise totally by 8km (5 miles) above Earth.

SPEED
Outside Earth's atmosphere, meteors travel at 210,000km/h (130,000mph).

FRICTION
When space debris—even an object **the size of a pea**—slams into Earth's atmosphere at this speed, the resulting friction generates heat that vaporises the debris and causes the flash of light that is the tail of a "shooting star."

"Meteor" refers to the tail.

"Meteoroid" is the space debris that is vaporised.

"Meteorite" is the name for a meteoroid that does not burn up but falls all the way to Earth.

Dad, how can you see **a pea** that far up in the sky?

What you see is the **tail.** It's only about 1m (3ft) wide, but it's a few kilometres long.

actual size of a typical meteoroid

Piping up

People are divided about the sound of bagpipes.
Be prepared to lose some friends (or to listen to their excuses
for not coming to hear your efforts).

&!

1 **Blow here**

2 **Squeeze here**

3 **Play notes here**

It's a difficult instrument.
These steps will help.

- Find an **instructor.**
- Before buying a whole set of pipes, just get a **chanter** (see below).
- **Listen** to different types of pipe music.
- **Practise!** Be patient. Practise again.

The main parts

DRONES

bass

inside tenor

outside tenor

Drone pipes produce the characteristic sound of the pipes — a harmonizing note that continues while the melody is played on the chanter.

Drones consist of two or more sections with sliding joints, so you can adjust the pitch.

The bass drone is usually pitched two octaves below the chanter.

BAG

The engine that drives the music. By blowing air into the bag, and squeezing your elbow against it, you force air through the chanter and drone pipes.

The bag is traditionally made from animal skin, and some still are, but synthetic materials are used more often now. This one is covered in tartan cloth.

CHANTER

The melody pipe. Best to get one with countersunk finger holes.

As well as Scotland, many other cultures have developed their own form of bagpipes.

Bulgaria — *kaba gaida*

France — *bagad*

Galicia — *gaita*

Germany — *huemmelchen*

Greece — *tsampouna*

Hungary — *duda*

Southern India — *sruti upanga*

Southern Italy — *zampogna*

Romania — *cimpoi*

Sweden — *säckpipa*

Turkey — *tulum*

Pakistan is the world's largest manufacturer of bagpipes. The instruments have been made there for over a century, and they are exported worldwide, even to Scotland.

Making glass

It's more than just blowing.

1 There are **four main ingredients** in glassmaking:

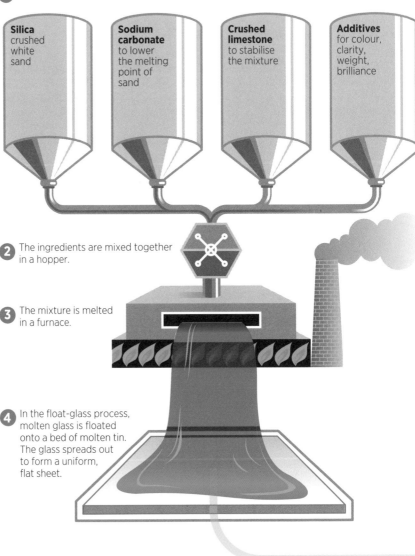

Silica
crushed white sand

Sodium carbonate
to lower the melting point of sand

Crushed limestone
to stabilise the mixture

Additives
for colour, clarity, weight, brilliance

2 The ingredients are mixed together in a hopper.

3 The mixture is melted in a furnace.

4 In the float-glass process, molten glass is floated onto a bed of molten tin. The glass spreads out to form a uniform, flat sheet.

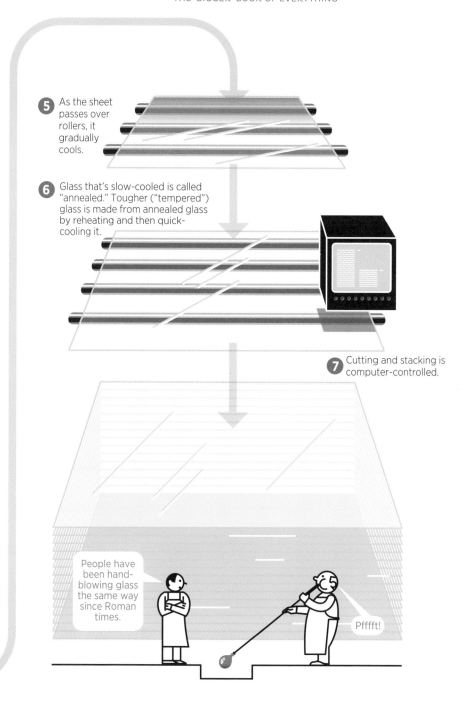

5 As the sheet passes over rollers, it gradually cools.

6 Glass that's slow-cooled is called "annealed." Tougher ("tempered") glass is made from annealed glass by reheating and then quick-cooling it.

7 Cutting and stacking is computer-controlled.

People have been hand-blowing glass the same way since Roman times.

Pfffft!

Finding places

Your **hotel concierge** is the **gatekeeper of the city.** He (or she) knows the top maitre d's, the hard-to-get ticket sources, the finest tailors—the best things their town has to offer.

How may I be of help?

ANY QUESTIONS?

Whether it's a simple request, such as finding the best parking spot or an almost impossible one, like arranging the aquisition and overseas shipping of an authentic London double-decker bus, it all comes down to the **address book.**

GOOD ANSWERS

But it's not just knowing the right people; a concierge must be quite the **know-it-all.*** When asked about the best bottle of whisky that money can buy, the concierge must be a single malt connoisseur. You want to rent a fast, luxury sports car? The good concierge knows the latest models and where they are available **beyond the usual** well-known rental-car companies.

LIKE TO TRY IT YOURSELF?

If you want to become a member of the prestigious French association **Les Clefs d'Or** (Golden Keys), you'll need at least five years' experience in the hotel industry, plus the backing of two current members, before going before a rigorous board review. There are approximately 4,000 members, worldwide.

Sight-seeing

Conc prior

Greater thread count

Drinks on the roof at midnight

*Seems like this book should be required reading for all concierges!

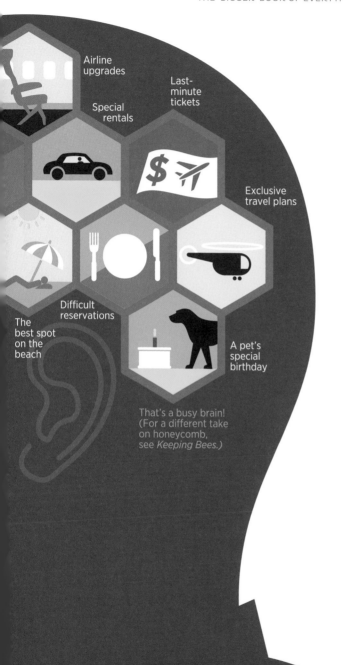

Airline upgrades

Last-minute tickets

Special rentals

Exclusive travel plans

Difficult reservations

The best spot on the beach

A pet's special birthday

That's a busy brain! (For a different take on honeycomb, see *Keeping Bees.*)

The best concierge...

HAS ORGANISING PRINCIPLES

With many customers to please—almost all of whom probably count themselves as rather more more important than anyone else nearby—a concierge must be **highly organised** in taking care of several unusual and time-sensitive requests all at once.

FINDS SOLUTIONS

We are all impatient. Being able to make a quick decision to fulfill the needs of the everyone and anyone is a big plus.

IS A MODEL OF DISCRETION

A conscientious concierge would never break the law for a guest. Pushing the law is a bit different. A good tip can go along way!

INDEX

INDEX

INDEX

WEBSITES

about.com; dotsub.com; electricaloutlet.org; paddling.net; wikipedia.org; wikihow.com; howstuffworks.com; desertmuseum.org; scientificamerican.com; fugufish.info; howany.com; icpri.com; sanfermin.com; squidoo.com; cio.com; yahoo.com; unhcr.org; wilderness-survival.net; howtoopenacoconut.com; polynesia.com; mosquitoworld.net; albanach.org; worldatlas.com; forbes.com; winearomawheel.com; mayoclinic.com; askmen.com; nih.gov; makemysushi.com; ehow.com; onthegotours.com; journeybeyondtravel.com; cnn.com; animaltourism.com; arachnophiliac.info; tramex.com; matadornetwork.com; survivalinternational.org

BOOKS

Rules of the Game, The Diagram Group • *The Worst-Case Scenario Survival Handbook*, Joshua Piven and David Borgenicht • *Jungle Survival*, UK Ministry of Defence • *Random House Encyclopaedia* • *The Riddle of the Rosetta Stone*, James Cross Giblin • USA Today Weather Book • *Rules of the Game*, The Diagram Group • AMA Encyclopaedia of Medicine • *The Human Body*, Charles Clayman (editor) • Northwoods Field Guides • *Mr. Beck's Underground Map*, Ken Garland • Edmund Scientific Star and Planet Locator • National Geographic Atlas of the World (9th edition) • *World Happiness Report*, John Helliwell, Richard Layard, Jeffrey Sachs (editors) • *Lonely Planet's Best Ever Travel Tips*, Tom Hall • *See Dad Cook*, Wayne Brachman • *Wordless Diagrams*, Nigel Holmes • *The Smallest-Ever Guide to Chocolate*, Nigel Holmes and Erin McKenna • *The Smallest-Ever Guide to Cocktails*, Nigel Holmes and Erin McKenna

ARTICLES IN THESE MAGAZINES

American History; Attaché; Backpacker; Business 2.0; Departures; eCompany Now; Field and Stream; GQ; Kid's Discover; Language Today; National Geographic; Navigator; Outdoor Explorer; Scholastic Scope; Sports Illustrated; Sports Illustrated for Women